T0182501

Witchy Cocktails

Witchy Cocktails

Over 65 recipes for enchantment in a glass, including classic cocktails, magical mocktails, pagan punches, and more

Cerridwen Greenleaf

CICO BOOKS
LONDON NEW YORK

For my truest love, Paul, who inspires me every single day.

Published in 2024 by CICO Books
An imprint of Ryland Peters & Small Ltd
20–21 Jockey's Fields, London WC1R 4BW
341 E 116th St, New York, NY 10029

www.rylandpeters.com

10 9 8 7 6 5 4 3 2 1

Some recipes in this book have been previously published by Ryland Peters & Small. See page 144 for full text and picture credits.

A CIP catalog record for this book is available from the Library of Congress and the British Library.

ISBN: 978-1-80065-380-1

Printed in China

Designer: Geoff Borin
Photographer: Stephen Conroy
Drink and prop stylist: Phil Mundy

Commissioning editor: Kristine Pidkameny
Art director: Sally Powell
Creative director: Leslie Harrington
Head of production: Patricia Harrington
Publishing manager: Carmel Edmonds

Notes

• Both imperial fl oz/US cups and metric measurements are included. Work with one set of measurements and do not alternate between the two within a recipe. All spoon measurements given are level: 1 teaspoon = 5 ml; 1 tablespoon = 15 ml.

• Uncooked or partially cooked eggs should not be served to the elderly or frail, young children, pregnant women or those with compromised immune systems.

• When a recipe calls for citrus zest or peel, buy unwaxed fruit and wash well before using. If you can only find treated fruit, scrub well in warm soapy water before using.

• To sterilize screw-top jars and bottles to store syrups, preheat the oven to 325°F/160°C/150°C fan/Gas 3. Wash the jars and/or bottles and their lids in hot soapy water, then rinse but do not dry them. Remove any rubber seals, then put the jars onto a baking sheet and into the oven for 10 minutes. Soak the lids in boiling water for a few minutes.

Contents

Introduction: Enchanted Cocktails and Magical Atmosphere

When I arrived in San Francisco years ago, shockingly, I was not yet drinking coffee and I had not yet had the experience of a crafted cocktail. I have always been a great lover of tea, and quite inadvertently, I was a teetotaller. San Francisco's vast array of classic bars and marvelous coffee shops lured me in and I gingerly began exploring. Within the first month of moving, I became a daily coffee drinker and have been starting my days with triple lattes for years now, oat-milled preferred.

One of my then new and now dear friends, Kimberly, loved the old-fashioned bars and lounges and charming oceanside joints in San Francisco's North Beach, which is how I came to discover the world of cocktails. One such place was the Persian Aub Zam Zam. Bruno, the late and great proprietor of this legendary establishment, was endearingly judgmental about what he served, preferring guests to order martinis. If you ordered something he considered beneath his dignity, he would instruct you to "go to the fern bar on the corner; we don't make that here." Luckily for me, my friend was aware of Bruno's rules so we knew exactly what to order. The décor of the Aub Zam Zam made you feel as if you had walked into an Arabian dream. Art and murals covered every inch of the small but well-appointed bar. While Sinatra and other members of the Rat Pack crooned softly in the background, it seemed like a beautiful dream.

I loved living in the San Francisco's fabled Haight Ashbury district, replete with charming small businesses, including the Aub Zam Zam. Right down the street, even closer to my humble dwelling, was a small shop, Curious and Candles. I was drawn in, literally, by the exotic incense they burned at all times. Once inside, I instantaneously felt at home. It was a tiny metaphysical store, but every inch was filled with witchy essentials, including crystals, jewelry, wands, books, tarot decks, posters, herbs, and everything you can imagine. A plentitude of curiosities! I was there every weekend and asked a lot of questions, which the patient and generous shopkeepers explained at length. Eventually, we became friends and I was invited to become a tarot reader at the shop if I passed muster with the owner. Thankfully, I did pass and became not only a tarot reader but also an astrological consultant for customers—I was in heaven!

After a Saturday shift in the store, Kimberly would pop over to peruse the shelves before the shop closed for the evening, and then we would walk up Haight Street, eager to compare notes on lore we had discovered. Often, we were studying a new astrology book and would have deep discussion of topics such as synastry (astrological compatibility), decanates (subdivisions of signs), and astrocartography (combining birth charts with geographical locations)—and we discovered that the Aub Zam Zam was the perfect setting for delving into these mysteries of the universe. The murals on the wall depicted Sufis and other seekers of answers to the meaning of life. Sipping one of Bruno's expertly crafted martinis was our companion on our journey into the supernatural.

My hope with this book is that one of these lovingly crafted cocktails may be the same for you, accompanying and inspiring your witchcraft. Whether you are seeking something to enjoy with a friend or partner, to sip solo, or to serve at a gathering of your coven, you will find the perfect recipe within these pages.

Chapter 1

The Magical Art of Witchy Mixology

Witchcraft requires certain tools for magical workings and the same is true for crafting witchy cocktails! I accumulate mine over time and still keep my eye out for charming cocktail accoutrements. Vintage bar tools are often the most charming of all. My pride is a set of astrological barspoons, one for each sign.

This section also offers a brief guide to some of the magical associations of the ingredients you will be using for these delectable libations.

Your Witchy Cocktail Toolkit

You may have a few essential bartending tools already, but you will doubtless need to acquire some more of them. I have found many of mine at yard sales for pennies. These lucky finds just need a good cleaning and cleansing to remove the remaining energy of those who used them before (see page 18).

The Basics

Barspoons: Proper stirring of cocktails cannot be accomplished with just any spoon—you need the longer, slimmer style.

Cocktail shaker: Many cocktails have several ingredients, best enjoyed by mixing with a good shake. Get a shaker that has a built-in strainer.

Jiggers: These, used by bartenders, are a must for measuring the exact amount of ingredients, which makes for a balanced cocktail. They are available in different sizes, ranging from ¾ oz (25 ml) to 1½ oz (45 ml) and 2 oz (60 ml).

Ice: Ice is an essential in many cocktails and mocktails. As well as cooling ingredients in a cocktail shaker and chilling glasses for greatest enjoyment of the drink, it can greatly enhance the tastes of certain recipes. One of my favorite uses for ice is with a neat shot of a great scotch or other liquor. First, taste the straight scotch in the glass and savor for a few sips. Then add one ice cube and taste. The difference in taste is remarkable—try it! I also suggest freezing fresh herbs in ice cubes to add a healing and savory note to your cocktails and mocktails. To make double-frozen ice, which takes longer to melt, freeze water in an ice-cube tray as normal; once frozen, allow it to thaw completely (which forces out any tiny oxygen bubbles), then re-freeze. Repeat this process for triple-frozen ice.

Other essential tools: A corkscrew, zesters and peelers, an ice bucket and ice pick, and kitchen cloths you can use as bar towels.

Glassware

The taste of your concoction will depend on the glass, so you will need to create a collection of barware. Very few of my cocktail glasses were purchased new; I picked them up for a few pence at thrift stores and the vintage designs add much charm. Some of them include:

Balloon/copa: This is a bulbous, rounded stemmed glass.

Collins: A tall and slim glass that can contain 10–14 oz (300–400 ml) of liquid, and used for a Tom Collins cocktail among others.

Coupe: A small bowl that is stemmed. It is used to serve cocktails such as daiquiris and an Aviation. You can also use it to serve Champagne.

Flute: A slim, fancy, long-stemmed glass, used for mimosas and Champagne. It can contain 6–10 oz (175–300 ml) of liquid.

Heatproof: For hot cocktails, heatproof glasses can be a stylish alternative to cups or mugs.

Highball: Akin to a Collins glass, the highball can contain 8–12 oz (235–350 ml) of liquid. It is used to mix and serve drinks such as iced tea drinks and tequila sunrise.

Hurricane: This glass looks a bit like an hourglass, inspired by hurricane lanterns used in storms.

Margarita: A margarita looks similar to a coupe glass, but contains two curves.

Martini: This glass features a V-shaped bowl. It is famously used to serve martinis with an olive pinned on a toothpick.

Rocks: Also called a lowball glass, a rocks glass is a short glass that can contain about 6–10 oz (175–300 ml) of liquid. It is used to serve whiskey or scotch with ice.

Shot glass: This is built for a one-gulp drink. It can typically hold ¾–1 oz (25–30 ml) of liquid.

Wine: Traditional wine glasses are also sometimes used for cocktails.

Bartending Know-how

When starting out making cocktails and mocktails, there may be terminology you are unfamiliar with. Here is a short guide to the art of making these delicious libations.

Shaking: The rule of thumb is to shake a cocktail for 15–20 seconds for a drink that will be served directly from the shaker. If it will be served in a glass with ice, shake for 5–7 seconds. Dry shaking simply means shaking the ingredients in the cocktail shaker without ice. Recipes which include egg whites for a frothing effect require a dry shake.

Muddling: This involves putting solid ingredients, such as slices of fruit and mint leaves, in a mixing jug or shaker, either on their own or with other ingredients, and then pressing/crushing them with the back of a barspoon or a "muddler" (a pestle). The idea is to release the fruit juices and the leaf flavors.

Straining and double-straining: Many cocktails have to be strained to ensure that solid ingredients and ice are not transferred from the shaker or mixing jug to the glass. If the cocktail only needs to be strained once, then a shaker with a built-in strainer will do the job. Double-straining is often necessary in cocktails, such as martinis, where the ingredients are shaken over ice but it is important to avoid even small shards of ice falling into the glass. The cocktail is poured through the strainer in the lid of the shaker, while a second, fine strainer is held over the glass.

Chilled glasses: Many cocktails in this book call for a well-chilled glass. One safe way to do this is to fill the appropriate glass with ice and leave until it feels very cold to the touch. Discard the ice before pouring the cocktail into the glass.

Twist: This usually refers to a strip of citrus peel, about 2 in. (5 cm) long. Cut the fruit in half at the middle. Use a paring knife around the edge to remove the peel, cutting away as much of the pith as possible. (It is easier if you use fruit with thick skins.) Remove the fruit and set aside. Cut the remaining peel circle so that it becomes a long strip. Twist it, holding it for several seconds until the shape forms.

Mist: Use a citrus peel to add a flavored mist. Hold the peel over the drink and twist, so that the oils in the peel are released in a fine mist that falls onto the surface of the drink.

Flaming: To do this, a piece of citrus peel is held at one end and a lighter brought up to it in order to release some of the oils. The peel is then held over the glass and twisted, to create a fine mist that falls onto the top of the cocktail (see Mist). The flaming produces a particularly aromatic mist.

Simple syrup: Simple syrup is one of the easiest-ever recipes: mix 1 part granulated sugar with 1 part water. You can heat the water and simmer until the sugar dissolves, then let cool, but some bartenders put the mixture in a cocktail shaker and shake until the sugar dissolves. Try both! If you make it ahead of time, it will keep for up to 1 month in a sterilized jar/bottle if refrigerated.

Salted and sugared rims: Some cocktails benefit from being drunk from a glass with the rim covered with a layer of salt or sugar (or, sometimes, with something more exotic, such as nutmeg or cocoa powder). First rub the rim of the glass with the cut side of a wedge of citrus fruit or with zest to create a sticky surface. (If you hold the glass upside-down, there is less chance of the juice running down the sides of the glass or into it.) Then dip the rim in salt or sugar on a plate or shallow tray. Shake off excess salt or sugar; none must fall into the glass.

Infusing: When a recipe includes an ingredient "infused" with a particular flavor, you can often buy the product ready-made. However, in some instances, you may have to do the infusing yourself. Generally, this is a simple matter of steeping the flavoring—strawberries, for instance—in the liquid, possibly sugar syrup, long enough for it to impart its flavor.

Essential Witchy Tools

The art of witchy cocktails calls for an extra dash of magic. As well as the items listed below, you may wish to keep other Wiccan elements close by for your magical workings, such as relevant crystals and images of deities.

Candles: These are truly essential. Follow your instinct on choosing sizes, shapes, and colors; keep an array of options on hand.

Incense: Incense contains inherent energies that you can use to further your intention and promote your purpose. Every New Age store, herb shop, or health food store has a wide variety of cone, stick, and loose incense. Powdered or loose incense needs to be burned on a charcoal cake, usually sold in these same stores in packets of ten. You should set the charcoals in a fireproof glass or clay dish or use your censer (incense burner) from which the smoke will waft out enchantingly.

Book of Shadows: This is a journal of your choosing in which you write down your magical workings, notes, and recipes. When you track the effectiveness of a ritual, you can use this to refine your spellcraft in the future and your power will increase. Record your incantations in your Book of Shadows and you'll soon learn which pairings of libations and enchantments are the most bewitching for you and your guests!

Athame: This magical knife should be placed on the right side of your altar. The athame (pronounced "a-thaw-may") is used to direct the energies raised in your ritual and usually has a dull blade. Since black is the color that absorbs energy, athames should have a dark handle.

Essential oils: These natural oils made by distillations of herbs and flowers, ideally organic, retain the fragrance of the original plant from which they are made. When you are making a blend of oils or a potion or lotion, mix them with a carrier (or base) oil, such as jojoba, almond, apricot, grapeseed, or sesame, to dilute the essential oil, making it safe to apply to the skin. Always test a blend on a small area of the skin first and leave for 24 hours to check you do not have any reaction to it.

Altar: Your altar is the center of your enchantments, your personal power space. A Wiccan altar is where you place symbolic and functional items for the purpose of spells and ritual work, as well as a space for speaking chants and prayers. You can have more than one altar, depending on its purpose, and even your cocktail-making area can become an altar for magical mixology (see page 16).

Cauldron: A cast-iron cauldron can hold fire and can even be used to burn incense or purifying sage. Place a cauldron on your altar if there is room, or on the floor to the left of the altar. Cauldrons represent the Goddess (also called Source or divine power), their round basins symbolizing the womb from whence all comes.

Turning Your Bar into an Altar

Consider what you want to evoke with your magical mixology. Conviviality, health, spiritual insight, and prosperity can all be enhanced by turning your bar into an altar.

Whether you run a pub or dazzle your guests with cocktails you whip up at home, the surface and area you use is your bar and, like any magical workspace, adding sacred elements will greatly enhance your craft as well as the art of creating consecrated cocktails. Because your bar needs to accommodate activity—mixing, shaking, stirring, blending, to name but a few—you should think more minimally in your approach than you would with a richly laden Wiccan altar adorned with many holy tools and *objets d'art*. You need to be able to move quickly without knocking anything over. Less can be more!

Like many others, my home is not large enough to have a whole room that serves as a bar. Instead, I use a counter in the kitchen to mix drinks and I also have a vintage bar cart, on which I've created a mini shrine by placing a beautiful tray on top of it. The bar cart is mobile, so it can be rolled into any area where libations will be served, including outdoors. Vintage bar carts can be purchased for a song and can be extremely charming with old-fashioned details.

I always keep an eye out for antique trays at thrift stores. This is an excellent way to get very high-quality goods for the lowest costs. Select a tray that can hold a few sacred objects, is pleasing to your eye, and seems special. It can be square, rectangular, or even round—let your feelings guide you on the choice.

Once you have landed on the ideal tray for your shrine, clean both the bar cart and the tray with the Purity and Prosperity Wash (see page 18).

SEEDLIP
GARDEN 108
FENTIMANS
PREMIUM INDIAN
TONIC WATER
FENTIMANS
PREMIUM INDIAN
TONIC WATER

Purity and Prosperity Wash

As with anything you buy at a store, you need to remove lingering energies, and this is especially true for anything you buy at a vintage shop, because these treasures had previous owners. This quick wash, which also has a very refreshing citrusy-sweet scent, will ensure your new discoveries will be imbued with the energy you wish to bring to your sacred space.

Pour 2 cups (500 ml) white vinegar into a large mixing bowl. Add essential oils—8 drops of lemon and 6 drops of lavender—plus 3 sage leaves, 3 cinnamon sticks, and 1 cup (250 ml) hot water, then let it steep for a half hour. Stir three times while the mixture steeps and cools. Remove the cinnamon sticks and set them aside to dry for the next stage of magical preparation (see below).

Dip a dishcloth into the mixture, wring it out so it won't drip, and lightly and carefully wipe the surface of the tray, bar cart, or table surface you are using for your magical mixology. Allow it to dry.

Supernatural Shrine

Complete the process of sanctifying your bar area with this short ritual, which harnesses the powers of several bringers of money energy and protection.

Place a pyrite crystal (also known as Fool's Gold) in the far-right corner of the newly cleansed tray—this is the prosperity area and the ideal placement for this powerful money magic stone. In front of the crystal, set vanilla incense in a fireproof dish. Place the cinnamon sticks you used in the Purity and Prosperity Wash with 3 leaves of fresh basil in a small green dish in the far-left corner. Set a votive candle in front of the green dish. Pour ½ cup (125 ml) water into a small green bowl and set it in the very front middle of the tray. Gently add a gardenia blossom so it floats on the water.

Now, light the candle, then light the incense with the flame of the candle. Say aloud:

Every brew made here will be a blessing.

Here will be served good health.

All here will be served good cheer.

Health and wealth and abundance, be here now and always.

So mote it be!

You are now all set to begin crafting cocktails!

Consecrating Your Tools

We Wiccans are well acquainted with the importance of having the right tools and of taking proper care of them. The same techniques for sanctifying your tools for the craft of Wicca can be used to great effect with your witchy cocktail kit.

Gather together a symbol of each of the four elements: a candle for fire, incense for air, a cup of water, and a bowl of salt (to represent earth). Light the candle and the incense. Take the new tool which is to be consecrated and pass it through the scented smoke of the incense, saying:

Now inspired with the breath of air.

Then pass the tool swiftly through the flame of the candle and say:

Burnished by fire.

Sprinkle the tool with water and say:

Purified by water.

Dip the tool into the bowl of salt and say:

Empowered by the earth.

Hold the tool before you with both hands and imagine an enveloping, warm white light purifying the tool. Now say:

Steeped in spirit and bright with light.

Place the cleansed tool upon your altar (see page 16) and say:

By craft made and by craft charged and changed, this tool I will use for the purpose of good in this world and in the realm of the gods and goddesses. I hereby consecrate this [name the tool here].

Magical Ingredients

Cocktails and mocktails are usually a mix of spirits, mixers, fruit, and herbs. Many of these ingredients have their own energies and can confer mystical meaning and power into your creations.

Fruitful Magic

While we often think of herbs and flowers as having special properties, it is much less commonly known that fruits also contain much magic you must try for yourself.

Apple: This "one a day" beloved fruit is associated with the goddess Pomona and contains the powers of healing, love, and abundance, Samhain, the high holiday of the Wheel of the Year, is also called the "Feast of Apples," as apples are used on the Halloween altar during this festival. Cutting an apple in half and sharing the other half with your beloved ensures that the two of you will stay happy.

Apricot: This juicy treasure is associated with Venus and the power of love, and it is believed that drinking the nectar will make you more appealing romantically. The juice of the apricot is used in rituals and love potions. Truly a food of the goddess!

Blackberry: Blackberries are the medicine that pops up anywhere, offering a delightful snack and serious healing, love, and abundance. Both the vine and the berries can be used for money-bringing spells. Thorny blackberry vines are wonderful as protective wreaths for your home, and the plant vine and berry can be used for prosperity and money spells.

Blueberry: These berries are almost like an evil eye made of fruit, as they offer great protection. You can tuck them under the mat at the threshold of your house to ward off negative vibrations.Blueberries are an aura brightener, with their brilliant blue color and affirmative energy. Easily grown, this fruit is one of the healthiest things you can eat and even adds to longevity. This sweet berry and the leaves from the plant also bring luck and prosperity.

Cherry: Beloved for their bright red color and taste, cherries are associated with romance, as well as powers of divination. Useful in love spells, the Japanese believe tying a strand of hair from your head onto the blossom of a cherry tree will bring a lover to you.

Grape: Planting grapevines grants abilities for money magic, as well as the joy of growing grapes. The ancient Romans painted pictures of grapes on their garden walls to ensure good harvest and fertility for women. For mental focus, eat some grapes. Magical spell workings for money are abetted greatly by placing a bowl of grapes on your altar (see page 16).

Lemon: This beloved member of the citrus family commutes the rare power of longevity as well as that of faithful friendship, purification, love, and luck. The juice from a lemon mixed with water can be used to consecrate magical tools and items during a full moon. Dried lemon flowers and peel can also be used in love potions and sachets. Bake a lemon pie for the object of your desire and he or she will remain faithful to you for all time. Imbibing lemon leaf tea stirs lust.

Orange: Like their joyful color, oranges are a fruit of happiness in love and marriage. Dried blossoms added to a hot bath will make you more beautiful. A spritz of orange juice will add to the potency of any love potion. Orange sachets and other gifts with this fruit offer the recipient utter felicity, thus it is an ideal gift for newlyweds.

Peach: Eating peaches encourages love, and they also enhance wisdom. An amulet made with the pit can ward off evil. A fallen branch from a peach tree can make for an excellent magic wand, while a piece of wood from a peach tree carried in your pocket is an excellent talisman for a long life.

Pineapple: Renowned as a symbol of hospitality, this fruit represents neighborliness, but also abundance and chastity. Dried pineapple in a sachet added to bathwater will bring great luck. Dried pineapple peel is great in money spells and mixtures.

Plum: Plums are for protection and add sweetness to romantic love. A fallen branch from a plum tree hung over the door keeps out negative energy and wards off evil.

Pomegranate: This fruit brings powers of divination, as well as engendering wealth. Eating the seeds or carrying the rind in a pocket sachet can increase fruitfulness in childbearing. Always make a wish before eating the fruit, for your wish will come true. Grenadine syrup (often used in cocktails) is derived from pomegranate.

Raspberry: This sweet berry has tremendous powers for true love and home safety. Hang the vines at doors when a person in the house has died so that the spirit won't enter the home again. The leaves are carried by pregnant woman to help with the pains of childbirth and pregnancy itself. Raspberries are often served to induce love, too.

Strawberry: This beloved fruit enhances health, wealth, and love. Strawberry leaves are carried for luck, and also help with childbirth.

Tomato: Remember that the tomato is a fruit! An easy money spell is to place a fresh-off-the-vine tomato on the mantle every few days to bring prosperity. Eating tomatoes inspires love. They are great in your garden as an aid to ward off pests of all kinds!

Magical Herbal Helpers

Herbs have many magical properties, which you can draw on in your cocktail making, as ingredients and garnishes, and in your other magical rituals.

Cinnamon: Refreshes and directs spirituality. It is also a protection herb and handy for healing, money, love, lust, personal power, and success with work and creative projects.

Lavender: A plant for happiness, peace, true love, long life, chastity, and is an excellent purifier that aids sleep.

Nutmeg: A lucky herb that promotes good health and prosperity and encourages fidelity.

Peppermint: An herb of purification, healing, and love. It supports relaxation and sleep as it helps to increase psychic powers.

Rosemary: Good for purification, protection, healing, relaxation, and intelligence. It attracts love and sensuality, helps with memory, and can keep you youthful.

Star anise: A lucky herb that aids divination and psychism.

Vanilla: Brings love and also enriches your mental capacity.

Spirited Spirits

Some of the most intriguing domains of the deities are those involving various nectars of the gods: alcohol. Always give thanks to the benevolent gods and goddesses from whom we enjoy such enjoyment. Cheers!

Bast: The Egyptian goddess of good health, Bast rules over not only cats but also wine.

Demeter: Our benefactor for whiskey and other grain-based draughts such as whiskey, rye, and bourbon is Demeter—thank her for all the bounty she provides.

Juno: Gin is made from juniper berries—the fruit of the guardian deity, Juno.

Maximon: When you are drinking tequila, agave, and mezcal, feel free to invoke Mayan god Maximon for guidance and abundance.

Pomona: Hard cider is a gift from the generous apple goddess, Pomona (see page 91).

Thor: Be sure to toast to thunder god Thor when you enjoy a mug of beer and he'll keep them coming.

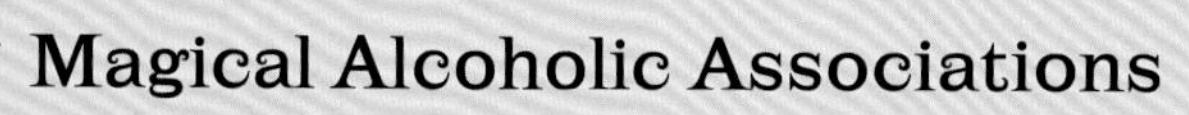

Magical Alcoholic Associations

Your choice of spirit can imbue your cocktail with even more magic:

Absinthe: brings out oracular abilities

Brandy: helps you find new love

Gin: abets the blessings of good health and longevity

Rum: offers protection

Tequila: helps with communication and inspires new ideas

Vodka: encourages perseverance

Whiskey: heart-healing, and attracts the positive good energy of fairies

A Spell in a Glass

As well as trying the spells and charms throughout the recipes in this book, you can also add enchantment to any cocktail or mocktail by performing an incantation while shaking the beverage in the cocktail shaker.

There is no need to burn incense or candles, as you do not want anything to compete with the charm-infused libation. Mix the drink as you normally would. When it is ready to be shaken, take the cocktail shaker and move it in a circle widdershins (counterclockwise). While shaking, speak this spell aloud:

With sacred intention, into this drink

I instill the energy of joy and love and pleasure.

Infused with the power of magic, into this glass,

I pour this spell. So mote it be!

You have now conjured a spell in a glass!

Chapter 2

Witchy Brews for Prosperity, Success, and a Happy Home

When you come home from work or an outing, your living space should create a special sensation as soon as you walk in: it should feel like a sanctuary, look beautiful to your eyes, and appeal to all your senses. Your home is your haven from the hurly burly of the outside world.

For witches, it is also your sacred space where you make magic. Creating specialty cocktails and mocktails are also magical workings, imbued with your intention; a spell in a glass. These recipes and rituals will help you augment and raise the energy of your home, ensuring that it is a place of great conviviality and good cheer, an abode filled with abundance, buoyancy, and sheer joy.

Margarita Money Mocktails

The prosperity of the ancient Aztecs was due no doubt in part to their use of agave, which is a plant that produces much luck and positive money energy. It also has healing properties and reduces inflammation and swelling, quickens the healing of wounds, and soothes the stomach. The Aztecs viewed it as a gift from the gods and I am in total agreement!

¾ cup (180 ml) fresh lime juice

⅓ cup (100 ml) fresh orange juice

⅓ cup (100 ml) light agave nectar

1 cup ice cubes

1 cup (250 ml) chilled lime seltzer

Garnish: lime twist

Serves 2

Mix the lime and orange juices and agave nectar in a jug, then pour into an ice tray with 12 compartments. Freeze for at least 5 hours or over overnight.

Put the lime seltzer, frozen cubes of citrus juice, and ice cubes into a blender, and blend on a high setting. When the mixture is smooth, pour it into margarita glasses with a salted rim (see page 13) and garnish with a lime twist. Perform the spell below before you enjoy the drink with a special person!

Quick Money Agave Spell

This ritual will not only bring you money quickly but also, as a bonus, takes very little time. Take a silver spoon and gently stir the cocktail widdershins (counterclockwise), saying the following words aloud:

To the gods of ancient times, to the goddesses of the present,

The sweetness of prosperity and security will flow to me until my cup runneth over.

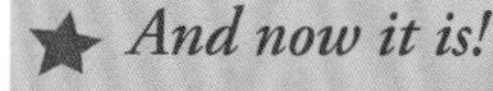

And now it is!

As you imbibe, repeat the words of the spell. Money will flow toward you! Be sure to thank the gods and goddesses for their munificence.

Uplift with Lemon: Self-care Scrub

This wonderfully simple scrub for you will fill you and your home with jollity thanks to the endorphine-inducing citrus scent. It is both a health and a mood booster. Mix ½ cup (100 g) white sugar, 2 tbsp lemon juice, 1 tsp lemon zest, and 1 tbsp olive oil together, then transfer to a sealable glass jar. Use when bathing. Rinse the tub and sink thoroughly after use. The scrub can be stored for up to two months. Add a lovely label to the jar to make a pretty and practical gift for a pagan pal!

Life Is Good Lemon Drop

Citrus brightens up any day—or night! A lemon-laden cocktail is guaranteed to confer a dose of vivacity and pure fun into any gathering, along with a sense of optimism and a sense that all is well. Life truly is good with lemon! A happy life is all about balance and the sweet and sour tastes of the lemon drop are the perfect flavor pairing.

2 oz (60 ml) lemon-infused vodka (see page 13)

1 oz (30 ml) fresh lemon juice

½ oz (15 ml) triple sec

1 oz (30 ml) simple syrup (see page 12)

Garnish: lemon twist

Serves 1

Add the vodka, lemon juice, triple sec and the simple syrup into a cocktail shaker. Add ice, shake until cold, then strain into a glass with a sugared rim (see page 13).

Long Island Iced Protection Tea

This potent pair of drinks should be imbibed at home where you can relax. Rum, one of the ingredients that makes this cocktail so flavorful and memorable, lends the energy of protection to you and your living space.

1 oz (30 ml) vodka

1 oz (30 ml) white rum

1 oz (30 ml) gin

1 oz (30 ml) tequila

1 oz (30 ml) triple sec

1 oz (30 ml) runny honey

1 oz (30 ml) fresh lemon juice

2 oz (60 ml) cola

2 lemon slices

Garnish: fresh mint

Serves 2

Pour the vodka, rum, gin, tequila, triple sec, honey, and lemon juice into a cocktail shaker filled with ice. Shake for about 15 seconds until well chilled. Fill two glasses with ice and lemon wheels. Strain into the glasses, then top with cola. Garnish with mint leaves.

Rum Ritual for Banishing

Rum has potency for warding off ill intentions coming toward you. Place a shot glass of white rum on your altar (see page 16) beside a candle. Anoint the side of the candle with a little rum (not near the wick, to be fire-safe). Light the candle and say aloud:

With these herbs, I cleanse my surroundings.

The negative forces aimed at me, begone.

Purified by fire, guarded by light.

This spirit protects me, dark energies shall flee!

So mote it be.

Extinguish the candle. Leave the rum on your altar for 24 hours to allow its protective energies to waft throughout your home. Afterward, pour the rum into the earth near your front door to ward off negative energy.

Rhubarb and Strawberry Fields Forever Collins

Strawberries are one of the sweetest things in life and in our romantic relationships. Long considered an aphrodisiac, these cheery fruits bring abundant health and wealth as well as bountiful love into your life!

1 rhubarb stalk, sliced

1 strawberry, cleaned and hulled

1½ oz (45 ml) silver tequila (the purest form of the blue agave)

⅓ oz (10 ml) agave nectar

¾ oz (25 ml) fresh lime juice

2 oz (60 ml) grapefruit soda

Garnish: rhubarb stalk

Serves 1

Muddle the rhubarb and strawberry in a cocktail shaker with a long spoon and a couple of shakes. Fold in the tequila, agave nectar, and lime juice, then add ice, seal up, and shake vigorously.

Strain the cocktail into a Collins glass filled with ice and with a salted rim (see page 13), leaving some room in the glass. Top the drink with the grapefruit soda. Add a rhubarb stalk to stir the cocktail, if you wish.

Strawberry Morning Meditation

For this meditation, you only need a handful of fresh, clean strawberries. Sit in a comfortable position, where you can see, and ideally feel, the warmth of morning sun and the glow. Close your eyes and, as you feel the sensation of the morning sun warming your skin, visualize yourself blooming and healthy, radiant with happiness, and beaming with joy. Sit for at least five minutes as you envision your blissful, soon-to-come future. Open your eyes and slowly eat the strawberries, taking time to truly taste the sweet fruit on your tongue. When done, bow to the life-giving sun.

Fortune's Favorite Manhattan

Vermouth is a cornucopia of herbs added to a base of wine. The distinctive taste comes from the spices and buds infused in the aged wine. These include wormwood, which suffuses vermouth with magical properties. In combination with whiskey and cherries added as a garnish, a Manhattan is a cocktail that bestows a lot of luck and good fortune.

2 oz (60 ml) rye whiskey

1 oz (30 ml) sweet red vermouth

3 dashes orange bitters

Garnish: cherry

Serves 1

Add all the ingredients to an ice-filled cocktail shaker and gently shake. Strain into a coupe glass. Garnish with a cherry.

Wormwood Divination

Wormwood (*Artemisia absinthium*) interacts with your consciousness and activates your ability to receive glimpses of the future. A simple wormwood steam can help you tap into your predictive abilities. Add ½ cup (15 g) dried wormwood to a boiling pot of water. Turn off the heat and let the aromatic steam rise. Take a scarf or towel and hold it over your head to use as a loose tent. At a safe distance from the warm water, lean your head forward over the pot and inhale the wormwood-steeped steam. Breathe in deeply and exhale slowly, repeating seven times. Your third eye should be opening a window into your future. Be sure to record all your intuitions, missions, and visions in your Book of Shadows (see page 15).

Rumtini Richness

Two things set this martini apart: rum and nutmeg. This cocktail surprises the palate and awakens the senses with the enlivening flavor of the nutmeg. It is a good idea to keep a whole nutmeg at the ready in your bar and coffee station at home.

1¾ oz (50 ml) unaged rum

⅓ oz (10 ml) dry vermouth

Garnish: twist of lime peel, grated nutmeg

Serves 1

Stir the ingredients in a mixing glass with ice before straining into a small, stemmed wine glass. Garnish with a twist of lime peel and a pinch of grated nutmeg.

Nutmeg Money Bag

Nutmeg is prized in money magic. You can create a lucky money bag with a whole nutmeg and a cinnamon stick broken into three pieces. Simply take a tiny cloth (such as muslin) bag that can be tied to close and place the spices in the bag. Close it securely and place it on your altar (see page 16) during the two days of a waxing moon. When this moon phase ends, place the money bag in your purse or pocket. By the next waxing moon phase, you will have more money!

Butterscotch Mocktail

I am an unabashed lover of vanilla. Here it is paired with butterscotch syrup to make an exceptionally sweet treat, which will engender much merriment and invoke the prosperity energy of the color green.

1 oz (30 ml) butterscotch syrup, such as Torani

¼ tsp vanilla extract

3 drops organic green food coloring

1 cup (250 ml) soda water

1 oz (30 ml) heavy (double) cream

Serves 1

Put the butterscotch syrup, vanilla extract, food coloring, and a dash of soda water in a beer mug and stir. Whip the heavy (double) cream and set aside.

Top up the mug with the soda water, leaving room to add a floating layer of the whipped cream.

Comfort and Joy Vanilla Candle

The smell of vanilla is so comforting and heartening. It is a scent that is instantly cheering and reminds us that life is, indeed, very sweet and filled with positive possibilities. Making candles can be greatly enjoyable, with yummy scents wafting throughout your home. This may well be the world's easiest candle to make!

Carefully melt 5 oz (140 g) beeswax in a double-boiler pan. Add 1 heaping tsp vanilla powder and 6 drops vanilla essential oil into the warm wax and stir using a wooden spoon. Add a wick at least 10 in (25 cm) long to the center of your chosen glass votive. (You could use an 8-oz (235-ml) clear rocks cocktail glass.) Secure the wick by bending it over the side of the glass. When the wax is all melted, take it off the heat and slowly pour it into the glass. The powder causes a pretty effect of flecks in the wax. Let the candle cool completely and then trim the wick to the right size—about ¼ in. (0.5 cm) long. You now have a simple and sacred vanilla candle that can bring you much coziness and imbue your home with vanilla-powered positivity.

Pumpkin Spice Prosperity Coffee

This delicious dessert drink infuses prosperity into your life with orange, clove, and pumpkin, which are all excellent ingredients for abundance. The combination of the coffee with warming brandy, fragrant orange, and comforting spices creates a delectable treat to share with good friends.

1 oz (30 ml) rum or brandy (100% proof/50% ABV)

⅔ oz (20 ml) orange liqueur (such as Grand Marnier)

1 oz (30 ml) oat milk

1–2 tsp (5–10 ml) pumpkin spice syrup

3 oz (90 ml) hot espresso coffee

Mixed spice

Garnish: orange wedge studded with cloves

Serves 1

Add all the ingredients to a heatproof pitcher/jug and stir together. Pour the hot coffee cocktail mixture into a warmed heatproof glass prepared with a sugared and mixed spice rim (see page 13). Garnish with the clove-studded orange wedge, and serve at once.

Invocation of Abundance

Before quaffing this coffee, a quick money spell will draw abundance toward you. Hold the pyrite from your shrine (see page 16) or another money magic crystal in your left hand and speak aloud:

Good luck and abundance, come to me fast.

There is plenty for all in the world, and as I receive, so shall I give.

Abundance for all is my wish. So shall it be!

Down the charmed coffee while the words are still in the air!

Aura-Cleansing Mystic Mojito

Blackcurrant leaves can be dried and sprinkled at doorways to protect and clear energy at your home as well as create a calm atmosphere. Utilizing the leaves in this drink can do the exact same things for your aura.

1 lime, cut into 6 wedges

5 small blackcurrant leaves, 3 whole and 2 finely sliced

1 tsp (5 ml) demerara (turbinado) sugar

¾ oz (20 ml) Wild Hibiscus Syrup (see below)

2 oz (60 ml) spiced rum

Soda water

Garnish: sprig of blackcurrant sage in flower, blackcurrant leaves, and hollyhock (*Alcea*) flower

Serves 1

Put 4 wedges of lime, 3 whole blackcurrant leaves, and the sugar in a Collins glass, and muddle. Add the Wild Hibiscus Syrup. Half-fill the glass with ice cubes. Add the rum, the remaining 2 lime wedges, and the 2 finely sliced blackcurrant leaves. Top with soda water and garnish with the sprig of blackcurrant sage flowers and blackcurrant leaves. You could add a hollyhock flower, too.

For the Wild Hibiscus Syrup: Add 1 cup dried hibiscus flowers, 1 cup (200 g) superfine (caster) sugar, and 1 cup (250 ml) water to a nonreactive pan and bring to a boil. Remove from the heat and let the ingredients steep for 20 minutes, then strain. Store in a sterilized glass in the refrigerator. It will keep for up to 2 months.

Enchanting Hibiscus

Hibiscus is prized for its healthful vitamin C content, as well its aphrodisiac qualities—it brings a heightened love vibration. This floral herb can also cause visionary dreams. Keep a dream journal on your nightstand after enjoying this Mystic Mojito, because you may have a prophetic dream about your future true love!

Manifesting a New Home Ritual

Almond trees—their leaves, nuts, and flowers—contain positive energy magic to bring wealth, accomplishments, and the acquisition of property, Almond is especially good at finding a new home. Take a yellow wax candle and use your athame (see page 15) to carve the words "new home" in the wax of the candle. Anoint the candle with three drops of almond oil. Light the candle and place it on your altar (see page 16). Repeat this ritual daily for three days. A great new home will be easily found now.

Strength-giving Almond Espresso Martini

Almond is a delightful flavor and it is very soothing to your mind and spirit. It also gives strength and endurance. Any challenges you face will be vanquished after this coffee cocktail!

¾ oz (25 ml) freshly brewed strong espresso coffee

1¼ oz (35 ml) vodka

⅔ oz (20 ml) almond liqueur, such as Amaretto Disaronno

½ oz (15 ml) coffee liqueur, such as Kahlúa or Tia Maria

Garnish: 3 coffee beans and toasted, flaked (slivered) almonds

Serves 1

Pour all the ingredients into a cocktail shaker filled with ice cubes and shake vigorously. Strain into a martini glass. Wait for the cocktail to "separate"—a foam will rise to the top and the liquid below will become clearer. Garnish with the coffee beans and almonds.

The Black Rose Inspiration

Could there be any more refreshing pairing than chilled rosé and ripe blackberries? This dreamy drink is a goblet full of relaxation that will also stimulate your taste buds with the simultaneous hits of tartness and sweetness. Awaken your senses with this delectable cocktail.

5 fresh blackberries

1 sugar cube (brown or white)

1 oz (30 ml) fresh lime juice

⅔ oz (20 ml) vodka

3⅓ oz (100 ml) fruity rosé wine

Garnish: lime slice

Serves 1

Put 4 blackberries and the sugar cube in a rocks glass and muddle until the berries are crushed and the sugar dissolved. Add the lime juice, top up the glass with crushed ice, and pour over the vodka and wine. Garnish with the remaining blackberry and a lime slice.

Beautiful Blessings

The enticing berries we all enjoy grow on flourishing blackberry vines, which have an inherent binding energy. You can bind your abundance to you and attract even more with this easy money spell. On a waxing moon morning, take a blackberry and muddle it in a cup. Take a small piece of paper and a pen with purple ink. Dip the pen in the fresh-made blackberry ink and write this money affirmation spell on the paper:

Abundance is mine: money comes to me easily.

I keep and grow my prosperity.

And so it is!

Place the note on your altar (see page 16) for a full waxing moon phase. Compost the berry in your garden or a potted plant for more bountiful energy.

Blackberry Bounty Bellini

What makes a Bellini unique is the large amount of a single fruit, usually peach. This berry-centric version is a fresh take that adds a tangy note to balance out the sweetness. Blackberries grow bountifully and are superb in money-drawing magic.

4 fresh blackberries

1 tsp white sugar

1 oz (30 ml) vodka

2 tsp fresh lemon juice

Chilled Prosecco, to top up

Garnish: fresh blackberry

Serves 1

Put the blackberries and the sugar in a cocktail shaker and gently muddle until pulped. Add the vodka and lemon juice to the shaker with a handful of ice cubes and shake until frosted. Strain into a flute and top up with Prosecco. Garnish with the remaining blackberry.

Coin of Silver Prosperity

Every part of the blackberry plant is useful in prosperity magic: the fruit, leaves, vines, and roots. Gather two blackberry leaves and wrap them around a silver coin. Speak the words of this spell, then tuck the coin into your wallet:

May my income grow as quickly as a blackberry vine;

May my coffers overflow with the positive currency.

As this coin of silver will multiply, so do blessings from the earth, planet of plenty.

All bounty shall be used for the good. So mote it be!

Kitchen Witch Berry Breeze

Strawberries and blackberries grow in both my front and back yards. It is utterly satisfying to walk outside, pick ripe berries, and eat them on the spot. This garden-fresh cocktail recreates that "life is sweet" moment.

5–7 mixed fresh berries, such as strawberries, raspberries, blackberries, and/or blueberries (depending on their size)

3 lime wedges

2 sugar cubes (brown or white)

1¾ oz (50 ml) vodka

Garnish: fresh berries, lime wedge

Serves 1

Put the berries and lime wedges in a rocks glass with the sugar cubes and muddle until the sugar has dissolved and the fruit has released its juices. Top up the glass with crushed ice, pour over the vodka, stir gently to mix, and then cap with more crushed ice. Garnish with a few berries and a lime wedge.

Long, Good Life Hedgewitch Spell

Blueberries bring luck and prosperity. This house protection spell will make sure you will enjoy a long good life in your home. Shortly after dawn, go outside your front door with a bowl heaped full of blueberries and intone:

No harm shall enter here.

Life is sweet here. Life is good in this home.

Health and gladness abound here. No harm shall enter here.

And so it is! Blessed be!

Walk back inside and eat one blueberry in every room. Once you have been throughout the house, set the bowl of berries on your altar (see page 16). When dinner is served that day, make sure all your loved ones eat some berries. Blessed you shall be!

Spell of Summer Peach Blossom

The flavor of a ripe peach is magical in and of itself, and in this cocktail it creates a sensation of being in an orchard during harvest season—like summer in a glass! Peach also confers longevity.

1 oz (30 ml) vodka

1 oz (30 ml) peach purée

⅓ oz (10 ml) crème de pêche (peach liqueur)

Chilled Prosecco, to top up

2 dashes peach bitters

Garnish: fresh peach slice, mint sprig

Serves 1

Add the vodka, peach purée, and crème de pêche to a cocktail shaker filled with ice cubes and shake to mix. Strain into a flute glass and top up with Prosecco. Add the peach bitters. Garnish with a peach slice and a mint sprig.

Peachy Life Talisman

Peaches are lauded for the efficacy in magical workings for love but are also potent in warding off evil and negative energy. A fallen peach tree branch makes for a wonderful wand to drawing magical circles, as well as for protection and directing energies. Put a clean, dry peach pit in your pocket and it will keep you safe from ill intentions and be a lucky talisman, bringing you success and a long, happy life.

Chapter 3

Love Potions: Aphrodisiac Cocktails

The concept of special libations for love has been with us through the ages. A thoughtfully crafted cocktail or mocktail with the right ingredients and magical intentions can indeed become your "Love Potion #9." What effects are you hoping for? Here we have drinks and non-alcoholic treats that can help you find new love, catch the eye of a crush, heal the hurts of romance gone wrong, rekindle a past passion, or deepen the bonds of commitment.

Rickey Romance Mocktail

The Rickey is a classic cocktail and this mocktail version is an equal delight. While oranges and lemons can be used in love spells, lime has a power all its own to attract a faithful partner. A loyal romance is the most satisfying partner of all.

½ oz (15 ml) fresh lime juice

½ oz (15 ml) simple syrup (see page 12)

1 oz (30 ml) tonic water

1½ oz (45 ml) seltzer water

3 dashes Angostura bitters

Garnish: lime slice

Serves 1

Fill a rocks glass with ice and pour in the lime juice and simple syrup. Stir to mix and slowly add in the tonic water and seltzer water. Top with the bitters, garnish with lime, and your sparkling mocktail is ready to be served.

Love Come Back Spell

Limes and the essential oil derived from this cheerful citrus fruit can also be used to bring someone back into your life. This spell produces a message within two weeks, so be ready to respond. All you need is lime essential oil and two fresh limes. Put two drops of the lime essential oil onto a cleen, dry cloth, then anoint the door jamb of your front door and bedroom door by gently dabbing the cloth onto them. Now take the two limes and cut them in half. Go outside to the walkway up to your front door or entrance and squeeze the juice on the sidewalk, while intoning:

Love, come back to me. Our love is strong and true.

Lover, come back to me now. And so it is!

Sidecar Seduction

This delightfully old-school drink has stayed the test of time because it is very satisfying and surprisingly refreshing. Cognac is a type of brandy and holds all the powers of enchantment that brandy has—which, in matters of the heart, is to help find a new love interest. The essence of orange amplifies the properties of this charmed cocktail. No wonder people have been drinking this for decades!

1½ oz (45 ml) cognac

¾ oz (25 ml) orange liqueur, such as Cointreau

¾ oz (25 ml) fresh lemon juice

Serves 1

Add the cognac, orange liqueur, and lemon juice into a cocktail shaker filled with ice and shake. Strain and pour into a martini glass with a sugared rim (see page 13).

Start visualizing the perfect partner, who is soon to manifest. Before quaffing the cocktail, whisper aloud:

New love, true love, I see you coming near.

True love, new love, I see you are right here.

And so it is—blessed be thee!

Make sure to always look your best when you step out from now on, as your new, true love will appear very soon.

Bedazzling Boulevardier

Try this take on the classic Negroni which uses bourbon instead of gin. A strong drink like this is perfect to enjoy together after a few pleasurable dates when it may be time for things to heat up!

1 oz (30 ml) bourbon

1 oz (30 ml) Campari

1 oz (30 ml) sweet vermouth

Garnish: orange twist

Serves 1 to share

Add the bourbon, Campari, and sweet vermouth to a large mixing glass filled with ice and stir until chilled. Strain the mixture into a rocks glass filled with ice. Garnish with an orange twist. Share the cocktail with your partner!

Lucky Shot at Love Spell

Bourbons and whiskeys have been used as a medicine for centuries to heal physical maladies, but it is often forgotten that they are effective in healing your heart, too. This spell will make room for a positive new relationship into your life. Place a bottle of bourbon and a shot glass on your altar (see page 16) for a night and a day. Before you go to bed, pour a shot into the glass and say these words, holding the glass in your hand:

As I let go of old hurts and sorry, I make peace with my past.

As I say goodbye to pain and sadness, I say hello to my happy future.

There is a great love for me waiting around the corner!

And so it is!

Now drink the shot of bourbon and say after:

So mote it be!

Bellini Bliss Love Potion

When I first tasted a Bellini, I thought it was so heavenly that it must have been a gift from the gods and goddesses—more specifically, a gift from Venus, the goddess of love. The simple recipe is a dreamy drink that will make you think romantic thoughts and get you in the mood for love—perfect for entertaining a special someone!

2 medium-size very ripe unpeeled white peaches, halved and pitted (or use 1 cup/250 ml peach nectar)

1 oz (30 ml) or more fresh lemon juice

1 oz (30 ml) or more simple syrup (see page 12)

750-ml bottle chilled Prosecco

Serves 6

Purée the peaches, lemon juice, and syrup in a blender. Taste and, if needed, add more syrup or lemon juice. Strain the blend into six flutes, then fill each with Prosecco. Place one of the flutes on your altar (see page 16) for the Venus ritual below.

Venus Vibrations: Offering to the Goddess of Love

It is important to show respect and appreciation to Venus for the help she gives us in our love life. You want to stay in her favor so you can call upon her when you need her aid. Say this prayer:

Venus, cast your light on me, a goddess for today I'll be.

A lover, strong and brave and true, I seek as a reflection of you.

And so it is!

Thank you for light and love, great goddess!

When the ritual is complete, the last glass of Bellini Bliss can and should be drunk!

Elderflower Enchantment

The blooming shrub elderflower is a very special herb; not only does it help attract new love, but it can also bring long and lasting love and faithfulness to your relationship and help a romance become a marriage. This flower of fidelity is one couples should share regularly and enjoy together. This combination of elderflower cordial and muddled fresh mint couldn't be more refreshing on a hot summer's day.

4 fresh mint leaves

¼ lime, cut into wedges

¾ oz (25 ml) elderflower cordial

Chilled Prosecco, to top up

Splash of soda water

Garnish: fresh mint

Serves 1

Put the mint leaves and the lime wedges in a large balloon/copa glass (or large wine glass) and gently muddle them. Add the elderflower cordial and a handful of ice cubes, and half-fill the glass with Prosecco. Stir gently, top up with Prosecco, and add a splash of soda water. Garnish with mint leaves.

Make it a mocktail: Simply replace the Prosecco with a sparkling alcohol-free wine.

Elderflower Commitment Rite

If you have been enjoying your elderflower cordial cocktail with your sweetheart, your relationship is doubtless getting more serious. This rite can sanctify your commitment to each other. Invite your loved one to share in this binding rite.

Anoint one red candle (signifying passionate love) and one pink candle (representing affection) with rose essential oil and place them a few inches away from each other on a table which will be your temporary love altar. Between them, place a small bowl filled with dried elderflowers. In front of the candles and bowl, place some rose or floral-scented incense in a fireproof dish. Light the candles and use a candle flame to light the incense. Set two Elderflower Enchantment drinks either side, away from any flames.

Before drinking the libations together, hold hands and speak the words of this spell:

On this bright day to mark our pledge, we choose each other from this day forward.

In this golden year, we pledge to each other to love, support, honor, and treasure our hearts.

Our love shines like the stars now and forever.

So mote it be!

Now drink the libations together as the romance-enhancing herb imbues you both with feelings of affection and lasting true love. When you have quaffed your drinks, extinguish the flames and keep the ritual elements in your bedroom as a small love altar, there for any time you want to renew your commitment to each other.

Martinis-for-Two Enchantment

This is the perfect cocktail to share for anniversaries or Valentine's Day and will make for an evening to remember. Adding rose, both in the liqueur or honey and the petals, infuses the martini with the essence of pure love. Keep the cork from the sparkling wine to use for a love spell (see below).

2 oz (50 ml) dry gin (ideally floral-forward) or vodka (milk-based)

½ oz (15 ml) fresh lemon juice

½ oz (15 ml) rose honey or rose liqueur

Chilled sparkling rosé wine, to top up

Garnish: rose petals (fresh or dried, but always food safe)

Serves 2

Add all the ingredients, except the wine, to a cocktail shaker and shake vigorously with ice. Strain and divide the contents between two glasses, before topping up with the sparkling wine. Garnish each drink with a rose petal.

Love Charm Box

A very simple way to preserve the effervescence of falling in love in your life is to make a charm box. It can be a literal small box or a jar with the lid; whatever container your eye prefers, as long as it can be sealed. Take the cork you saved and put it in the container you've chosen, along with a palmful of pink rose petals, two pieces of rose quartz, and two copper pennies. Keep it in your bedroom and the sweet little charm box will act like a battery, exuding the vitality of new love in your personal space and making it accessible to you at all times.

Whisky and Fuji Apple Love Spritzer

Apples are abundant with love and can bring the energy of romance, sweetness, and bliss. If you have never had a Japanese Fuji apple before, then it is worth making this drink and the one on page 66 just to try this amazing fruit! The skin can range from white to the deepest of pinks, and it has a unique floral taste.

1¼ oz (35 ml) Japanese whisky

2½ oz (75 ml) freshly pressed Fuji apple juice (extracted with a juicer from 1–2 apples), plus 1 whole apple

Garnish: Fuji apple slices

Serves 1

Add the whisky to a highball glass full of ice. Pour the pressed juice through a sieve/strainer into the glass. Garnish with Fuji apple slices. Keep one apple whole and set it aside for the spellwork below.

Conjuring True Love

Take the apple you set aside and hold it in your left hand while you speak these words aloud:

Love grows in my heart: I feel it in the core of my being.

As my vibration soars higher, love grows in my life.

My truest love comes to me now—enveloping me and surrounding me, every day for now and all time.

And so it is!

Eat the apple, keep the core, and bury it in your backyard or within a large potted plant. As the apple returns to the earth, nourish the soil, so your new love will nourish your soul.

Fairy's Favorite Apple Spritz

As well as being a fruit of love, apples are a favorite fairy food! This non-alcoholic version of the Whisky and Fuji Apple Lover Spritzer (see page 64) is a libation that will please the wee ones and fetch the blessings of the fairy realm.

⅔ oz (20 ml) Fuji Apple Cordial (see below)

2½ oz (75 ml) freshly pressed Fuji apple juice (extracted with a juicer from 1–2 apples)

1¾ oz (50 ml) soda water

Garnish: edible flower

Serves 1

Add the apple cordial to a highball glass full of ice. Sieve/strain the juice into the glass. Top up with soda water and garnish with an edible flower.

For the Fuji Apple Cordial: Extract the juice of 4 Fuji apples in a juicer and strain through a coffee filter. Weigh the juice, then measure out 40% of that weight in caster/granulated sugar and 1% in malic acid and stir in until dissolved. Bottle in a sterilized jar and store the cordial in the refrigerator for up to 1 month.

Cauldron Conjuration: Brewing Up Love

By brewing apples, you will send the fragrant scent of the fruit wafting throughout your home and fill it with the essence of love.

Fill a medium-sized pan to act as a cauldron with 2 quarts (2 liters) freshly drawn water, then add ¼ cup rose petals. Peel 3 apples and add the peels into the pan. (Set the peeled apples on your kitchen table to enjoy later.) Move the pan to the stove and turn the heat on low. Using the peeler, tear bits of scentful and spicy ginger root into the pan. As the mixture warms up, add in 4 sticks of cinnamon and ¼ cup (20 g) ground allspice. Stir 3 times widdershins (counterclockwise) with a wooden spoon.

Turn the stove down to a low simmer as the pure and positive energy of love fills your personal space. Sit down at your kitchen table and as the love magic brews, meditate and breathe in the redolent aroma, the perfume of love energy from the apple spice brew. Visualize the love flowing toward you, into you, and all around you. Now eat some of the peeled apples and, in so doing, you will also quite literally take the love energy into your body.

After about a half hour, turn the stove off and let the mixture cool. You can heat it one more time for a second infusion of love energy.

When the brew is completely cool, take it outside and pour the brew into the roots of any large shrub, garden, or lawn near your front door to instill the entry of your home with the upliftment of love.

Drink of Determination: Moscow Mule

The "mule" in this cocktail's name is indicative of the magical property of vodka itself, which is to persevere, no matter what. When you need a bracing drink during difficult times, turn to this cocktail, which will help you access your inner grit and determination. If you just went through a breakup, this is the drink for you!

2 oz (60 ml) vodka

½ oz (15 ml) fresh lime juice

3 oz (90 ml) chilled ginger beer

Garnish: lime slice

Serves 1

Fill a highball glass with ice, then add the vodka and lime juice. Top it with the ginger beer. Garnish with a lime slice.

Freya Invocation Ritual

After a bad breakup, or when facing any kind of adversity, in addition to making this cocktail, you should also pray to Freya, the Norse goddess who can send you both courage and encouragement. Hold a quartz crystal in your hand and pray aloud:

Great goddess of the North, Freya, I lay my burdens here today.

Please guide me to the best way through and beyond these troubles.

Thank you, Freya, oh goddess of endless wisdom.

Place the crystal on your altar (see page 16) and keep it there for a week. Your prayer will be heard and your struggles will begin to ease. Be sure to thank Freya for her help.

Supernatural Spicy Chai Chocolate

If you are in the early stages of a crush and want to speed things up, brew this luscious chai chocolate confection and share it with the object of your affection. You will soon have a budding romance (and more) on your hands!

12 green cardamom pods

1 tsp superfine (caster) sugar

1 cinnamon stick

1 pinch of freshly grated nutmeg

2 cups (500 ml) milk

1 tsp rose extract, rose water, or rose syrup

3½ oz (100 g) white chocolate, chopped

Garnish: freshly grated nutmeg

Serves 2

Begin by removing the black seeds from 2 of the cardamom pods and grinding them to a fine powder with the sugar using a pestle and mortar. Place the ground cardamom and remaining pods in a saucepan with the cinnamon stick, nutmeg, and milk, and bring to the boil over a low heat. Remove from the heat and leave the spices to infuse for 15–20 minutes, then discard the whole pods and cinnamon stick.

Add your chosen rose flavoring and the chopped white chocolate to the pan and return to a simmer over a low heat, whisking all the time, until the chocolate has melted. Pour into 2 cups or heatproof glasses. Garnish with a sprinkle of nutmeg.

Cardamom Seed Sensuality

Cardamom has been revered as a potent aphrodisiac by witchy women for millennia. Keep a dish of cardamom seeds on your nightstand. When you are preparing for an amorous evening, chew at least six of the cardamom seeds and your body will begin to become suffused with a pleasing heat and sensuality. This cherished spice will gently light the flame of passion to share with your partner.

A Toast to Friendship Spell

Agape, the kind of love friends enjoy, is considered the highest form of love, that of the gods and filled with empathy and understanding. When you invite your pagan pals over to share an evening of ritual and feasting, this sanctifying spell will multiply the blessings tenfold. After you serve cocktails to those who are gathered, say these words out loud:

Before the gods and goddesses we gather to celebrate our bonds,
our hopes for each other to prosper. our belief in each other's bliss!

Long may we live, love, and share all the blessings the deities have given us.

With grace and gratitude, so mote it be!

Fantasy Float

This red wine float offers a surprising twist on the classic whiskey sour. This is such an unusual cocktail that it should be reserved for a singular evening when you want to surprise and delight someone special.

1⅔ fl oz (50 ml) Bulleit Bourbon

¾ fl oz (25 ml) fresh lemon juice

¾ fl oz (25 ml) simple syrup (see page 12)

1 dash Angostura bitters

⅔ fl oz (20 ml) egg white

¾ fl oz (25 ml) red wine

Garnish: edible flower

Serves 1

Combine the drink ingredients, except the wine, in a cocktail shaker and "dry" shake without ice which will emulsify the egg white. Add a scoop of cubed ice and then shake vigorously. Strain into a small wine glass over cubed ice. Now pour the red wine, slowly and carefully over the back of a barspoon to float a layer of red wine over the cocktail. Garnish with an edible flower.

True Blue Hawaii

This dreamy cocktail represents the best of what life, and love, has to offer. Blue is the color of loyalty, which is desired in love relationships. Imbibing this brilliantly hued beverage symbolizes long-lasting love.

1 oz (30 ml) vodka

1 oz (30 ml) white rum

¾ oz (25 ml) Blue Curaçao

2 oz (60 ml) pineapple juice

½ oz (15 ml) fresh lime juice

½ oz (15 ml) fresh lemon juice

½ oz (15 ml) simple syrup (see page 12)

Crushed ice

Garnish: cocktail cherry, pineapple wedge

Serves 1

Pour the vodka, rum, Blue Curaçao, pineapple juice, lime and lemon juices, and simple syrup into a cocktail shaker. Add 2 palmfuls of ice and shake until everything is sufficiently cool. Strain the mixture into a hurricane glass filled with crushed ice. Garnish with a cherry and a pineapple wedge.

Love Note Rite

Curaçao's primary ingredient is orange, a fruit brimming with optimism and verve. Place two oranges on your altar (see page 16), one to represent you and one to represent your romantic partner. Write your hopes and wishes for a long, happy love with your partner and fold it. Place a shot glass filled with Blue Curaçao between the oranges on your altar. Tuck the love note under the glass. Leave these ritual elements in place for one day and one night. Notice as the bonds of love deepen and become even more true blue.

Bewitching Chocolate-lime Margarita

This dessert drink is redolent of romance with a touch of both sugar and spice. The chocolate liqueur and shavings are luxurious and the taste says "life is good, life is sweet!"

1¾ oz (50 ml) blanco tequila

½ oz (15 ml) fresh lime juice

¼ oz (10 ml) Cointreau

¼ oz (10 ml) crème de cacao (chocolate liqueur)

Garnish: dark chocolate shavings

Serves 1

Shake the ingredients vigorously with ice and fine-strain into a stemmed glass with a rim of chocolate shavings (see page 13).

Sweetness of Life Love Spell

Lore of chocolate indicates that the ancient Aztecs were the first to embrace the power and magic of chocolate and utilized the healing properties as well as the spiritual. They would combine chocolate with psychedelic mushrooms for shamanic rites. Aztecs also treasured chocolate as an aphrodisiac.

Take the chocolate bar you used for the cocktail garnish and divide it into two halves. Save it to share it with your beloved on a special night. To imbue the chocolate with additional power, speak this spell:

When we are together, every sense is awakened,
every feeling is heightened.

This sweetness we share is a sign of the bliss to come.

Together we experience the sweetness of life and love.

So mote it be!

Chapter 4

Medicinal Mixology

Centuries ago, village healers and herbal witches used certain fermented brews to tend their neighbors, families, and community, and when alcohols, such as whiskey, became more widely available, they were prescribed to patients well into the previous century; so, bitters, whiskey, and other fermentations have long been helping to heal many maladies and remain in use. They can provide a boost of energy and a lift to your spirits. As many a bartender has toasted while serving, "Here's the cure to what ails you!"

Grounding Grasshopper

Mint, particularly peppermint, is very much in alignment with the energy of sacred self-care. This long-beloved and very useful herb has a twofold effect in that it is both uplifting and calming—making it perfect for stress management! This soothing herb is especially good for our nervous systems and overall health.

1½ oz (45 ml) crème de cacao (chocolate liqueur)
1½ oz (45 ml) crème de menthe (mint liqueur)
2 oz (60 ml) heavy (double) cream

Garnish: shaved dark chocolate
Serves 1

Put all the ingredients into a cocktail shaker, add 2 palmfuls of ice, and shake until cold. Strain into a coupe glass. Garnish with chocolate shavings.

Crystal Visions Spell: Minting Tranquility

Modern life has us all on the run! We need to make sure creating calm is a major part of our self-care routine. This soothing spell will abet a sense of inner calm. Take your Grounding Grasshopper drink, a favorite candle, and some matches, and sit somewhere comfortable in your home with a table beside you. Place the candle and the libation on the table. Light the candle. Say these affirming words:

I am centered and at peace.
Surrounded by blessings, I find my serenity.
I claim my calm. All is well in my world.
Blessed be!

Now enjoy your drink and be sure to drink every last drop. As you sip, feel a sense of calm envelop you and infuse you with stillness and contentment. When the drink is finished the spell is done. Extinguish the candle and place it on your home altar (see page 16) for a boost of tranquility in your busy days.

Psychic Awakening Rosemary Milk

Rosemary, a gardener's favorite, has been prized for millennia for the many healing properties it offers, including how it aids memory and acts as an overall stimulant for our brains. This milk is excellent to sip before meditation to awaken your intuition and psychic powers.

2 cups (500 ml) milk

2 large fresh rosemary sprigs, washed

1–2 tsp runny honey, to taste

Serves 2

Put the milk in a saucepan. Crush the rosemary sprigs firmly with the flat blade of a large palette knife and drop them into the pan. Heat the milk very gently over a low heat until it just reaches boiling point. Remove from the heat and let it sit so that the rosemary can infuse for 5 minutes as it cools.

Sieve/strain the milk, discarding the rosemary, and pour into 2 heatproof glasses or cups. Add honey to taste and stir.

Mindful Moment

Take a sprig of fresh rosemary and crush it in your palms, then breathe in the enjoyably strong scent and clear your mind. Pay attention to what comes to your mind at the end of your mindful moment; it will be an important message just for you.

Infusion Inspiration

Cucumbers relieve inflammation, which is one of the reasons they are so marvelous for soothing skin and maintaining a youthful glow. Increase that effect even further with cucumber-mint water, which is hydrating and tasty, and will create a sense of well-being.

6 cups (1.4 liters) still water

2 large cucumbers, sliced into thin medallions

⅓ cup (10 g) fresh mint leaves

Serves 2

Pour the water into a pitcher with a lid and add the cucumber slices and fresh mint leaves. Close the pitcher and refrigerate overnight. Start your morning with this cooling refresher!

Hedgewitch's Garden Spritzer

Herbal healers centuries ago discovered that cucumbers are marvelously restoring for the skin. This reviving spritzer will feel like a glow-up! Plus, the combination of cucumber and mint has such a refreshing aroma that it will cool you down even before you take your first sip.

3 thick slices of cucumber

1 tsp fresh lemon juice

1 tsp white sugar

4 fresh mint leaves

Chilled Prosecco, to top up

Garnish: fresh mint, fine slice of cucumber

Serves 1

Put the cucumber, lemon juice, sugar, and mint leaves into a cocktail shaker and muddle well. Add a handful of ice cubes and shake vigorously. Strain into a large balloon/copa glass (or large wine glass) and top up with Prosecco. Garnish with a few mint leaves and a fine cucumber slice and serve at once.

Alabama Hedgewitch Healer

Sloe gin contains the fruit of the blackthorn tree, beloved by druids who used the essence of blackthorn to ward off bad energy and bad health. Blackthorn fruit was also viewed by hedgewitch healers to be a greatly useful healer of wounds both psychic and physical.

1 oz (30 ml) Southern Comfort

1 oz (30 ml) Amaretto

1 oz (30 ml) sloe gin

3 oz (90 ml) fresh orange juice

Garnish: orange wedge, cocktail cherry

Serves 1

Pour the Southern Comfort, Amaretto, sloe gin, and orange juice into a cocktail shaker, fill with ice, and shake until cold. Strain the cocktail into a highball glass filled with ice, and garnish with an orange wedge and a cocktail cherry.

Paradise Found Apricot Infused Oil

The Alabama Hedgewitch Healer cocktail lends an extra boost to health with the Amaretto liqueur, which contains not only the well-known almond but also apricot. Apricot, with its distinctive scent and appealing flavor, is very hydrating and good for your skin and overall vitality. For an oil to use in wellness rituals, add 4 clean apricot kernels, or pits, into a vial of ½ oz (15 ml) rose oil. Let the mixture steep in a dark, cool closet for one month. You will then have an oil that will conjure the fragrance of paradise itself!

Heavenly Hurricane

This fruit-forward favorite libation is redolent of southern climes and wild wet weather. Grenadine is derived from the richly red-hued pomegranate, adding a tangy top note and the gorgeous color.

1½ oz (45 ml) passion fruit syrup

1 oz (30 ml) fresh lime juice

1 oz (30 ml) fresh orange juice

2 oz (60 ml) light rum

2 oz (60 ml) dark rum

½ oz (15 ml) grenadine

Garnish: orange wedge, pomegranate peel twist

Serves 1

Pour all the ingredients into a cocktail shaker, fill with ice, and shake until cold. Strain the cocktail into a hurricane glass. Garnish with an orange wedge and a pomegranate peel twist.

Pomegranate Seed Soothing Meditation

The pomegranate fruit is rich in myth and legend and is also known for its healing properties, including being anti-inflammatory and filled with antioxidants. Simply eating the seeds is a real boost to your brain. Take a few pomegranate seeds for a sacred snack and sit in a comfortable place to meditate. Once you are settled, take three deep breaths and say aloud:

My peace is precious.

As I center here and now, I breathe in tranquility and release worry and stress.

Calm and serenity are mine.

Blessed be!

Take another three deep breaths, inhaling and exhaling slowly and calmly. Eat the pomegranate seeds, and as you do so, visualize the near and far future, filled with good, healthy, inspired ideas and sheer joy.

Restorative Mar-tea-ni

You can determine the desired medicinal effect of this clever cocktail by picking the type of tea used (see below). Vodka is derived from plants as well—namely potato and cereal grain—making this a nature-blessed beverage you can customize to your pleasure.

1 tea bag of your choice

1¾ oz (50 ml) vodka

⅓ oz (10 ml) Lillet Blanc (or Bianco Vermouth)

Garnish: lemon peel twist

Serves 1

Infuse the tea bag in the vodka for 60–90 seconds and then stir with the vermouth over ice. Strain into a glass teacup. Garnish with the lemon peel twist.

The Healing Magic of Tea

This drink allows a lot of room for innovation, as the tea that you use makes a massive difference to the cocktail. Peppermint, for example, adds a cool mint freshness, as well as soothing tummy discomfort and cleansing. Some other possibilities and their medicinal uses are:

- Chamomile: Helps with sleep and is good for abundance.
- Echinacea: Lends an increased and consistent sense of well-being, and prevents colds and flu.
- Fennel: Awakens and uplifts, freshens the breath, and aids colon health.
- Ginger root: Calms and cheers while aiding digestion, nausea, and circulation.
- Nettle: Raises the energy level, boosts the immune system, and is packed with iron and vitamins.
- Rose hip: Halts colds and flu and is packed with vitamin C.

Chi Chi Cheer

When you are enjoying a Chi Chi, you can taste the glamor of old Hollywood, where it was first made by Donn Beach. This recipe is a breeze to make. The ingredients contain the essence of island trees, coconut and pineapple—Mother Nature's bounty!

½ cup (70 g) frozen pineapple chunks

1½ oz (45 ml) vodka

1 oz (30 ml) coconut cream

4 oz (120 ml) pineapple juice

Garnish: pineapple slices

Serves 1

Pour all the ingredients into a blender and blend until it seems well mixed. Pour into a tiki mug, if you have one, or a goblet. Garnish with a pineapple slice or two to fully enjoy this tropical treat.

Coconut Body Blessing

Coconut is a purifier, both for your body and your spirit. This quick healing ritual will restore you each time you enact it. You will need 1 cup (250 ml) coconut water and some coconut oil. Pour the coconut water into a clear glass. Hold the glass in both hands and pray aloud:

We all come from the ocean and to her, we shall return.

Every drop of this elixir restores me; every cell of my being is healed.

I thank you, great mother goddess, for the gifts of life and the gift of love. So mote it be!

Drink a few sips of the water. Now take the coconut oil and apply it gently to your skin, over as much of your body as possible. Enjoy the rich scent of the coconut oil as it replenishes your body and your spirit. Thank the goddess again. We owe everything to her.

Pomona's Medicinal Appletini

This cool and crisp cocktail reminds me of the "apple a day" expression, but I will stop short of recommending an appletini a day to keep the doctor away. However, your physician might heartily approve of this as a choice of cocktail. It enlivens your senses at the first sip.

1½ oz (45 ml) vodka

¾ oz (25 ml) fresh lemon juice

⅔ oz (20 ml) sour apple liqueur or green apple schnapps

¾ oz (25 ml) simple syrup (see page 12)

Garnish: green apple slice or fan

Serves 1

Add all the ingredients to a cocktail shaker with a handful of ice cubes. Shake vigorously and strain into a chilled martini glass. Garnish with an apple slice or fan and serve.

Orchard Goddess Ritual

The apple is a beloved fruit which has the blessings of the lesser-known goddess Pomona and contains the powers of healing, love, and abundance. A simple way to show reverence to Pomona is to keep a bowl of apples on your altar (see page 16), or give thanks to her with this spell. Place an apple on your altar, light a green candle, and say aloud:

Goddess of the fields and orchards, I thank you for your beneficence.

You help feed the world.

Today, I will eat this apple in your honor.

Gratitude to you for all time. Blessed be thee!

Continue standing at your altar and eat the apple while you gaze at the flame of the green candle. When the apple is finished, the ritual is complete.

Best-Ever Breakfast Martini

The surprising addition of marmalade garnered the whimsical name for this cocktail. Marmalade is, of course, akin to jam and largely comprises orange and other citrus fruits, but always has the sunny taste of sweetened citrus.

2 oz (60 ml) gin

½ oz (15 ml) fresh lemon juice

1 heaped tsp marmalade

Serves 1

Add the ingredients to a cocktail shaker and shake vigorously with ice. Fine-strain into a V-shaped cocktail glass.

Supernatural Citrus

The citrus family offers some of the most uplifting energies of all. The essential oils, incenses, and candles made from these cheery and luminous scents are major mood shifters and can banish negative energy and bad moods.

• Lemon essential oil commutes the rare power of longevity, as well as that of faithful friendship, purification, love, and luck.

• Mandarin essential oil brightens moods and emotions and alleviates stress and insomnia. It can help you reconnect with your inner child.

• Orange essential oil added to a hot bath creates beauty, and a few drops of this oil will add to the potency of any love potion.

• Tangerine essential oil can be used to support the immune system, boost moods, and bring a clear mind.

Sweet Secrets Millie

This bold and spirited cocktail is unabashedly dessert-like. The recipe makes use of marmalade, just as in the Best-Ever Breakfast Martini (see page 92), but with the addition of new-make spirit. New-make spirit is essentially whiskey before it is aged. Depending upon the grains and yeast used, the flavors can vary greatly.

2 oz (60 ml) new-make spirit or white whiskey

½ oz (15 ml) fresh lemon juice

2 heaped tsp marmalade

Garnish: shortbread finger (optional)

Serves 1

Add the ingredients to a cocktail shaker and shake vigorously with ice. Fine-strain into a V-shaped cocktail glass and garnish with a shortbread finger on the side.

Whiskey Ritual

My husband's grandmother had one small tipple every night after dinner was served and all the evening chores were done. She had a shot of whiskey, but she savored it and made it last, warming in the glass in her hand. She lived to 108 years old so we might well say her evening treat was medicinal indeed. For this brilliantly simple rite, all you need is a shot of whiskey. Pour yourself a shot and say aloud:

As the gods watch over me, I ask for their blessing, and for health, love, and prosperity.

For everything you give, I am grateful. A toast to the gods!

So mote it be!

Then sip and savor the whiskey.

Greenwitchery Strawberry Mule

This mule is a gardener's delight and any fan of strawberries will exult in this distinctive approach to the classic mule cocktail. Ginger beer is an equal contributor to what makes this special and a beverage with benefits.

2 thin slices of peeled fresh ginger

3 fresh strawberries

1¾ oz (50 ml) vodka

½ oz (15 ml) crème de fraise des bois (strawberry liqueur)

1 dash simple syrup (see page 12)

Chilled spicy ginger beer, to top up

Garnish: fresh strawberry, lime zest

Serves 1

Put the fresh ginger and strawberries in a cocktail shaker and crush with a muddler. Add the vodka, crème de fraise des bois, and simple syrup. Add a handful of ice cubes, shake sharply, and strain into an ice-filled highball glass. Top up with ginger beer and stir gently. Garnish with a strawberry and lime zest.

The Splendor of Ginger

Ginger is known to alleviate indigestion, general nausea, an upset tummy, and a sore throat—it is a good addition to a hot toddy for cold symptoms. Ginger tea tastes very pleasant: you can buy tea bags or gently boil slices of fresh ginger root.

Herbal tea conjures a very powerful alchemy because when you drink it, you take the magic inside yourself. For an ambrosial brew with the power to calm any storm, add a sliver of ginger root and a pinch each of dried chamomile and peppermint to a cup of hot black tea. Before you drink, pray:

This day I pray for calm, health, and the wisdom to see the beauty of each waking moment.

Open Sesame

This creative cocktail is like a trip to the spa: revitalizing, rejuvenating, and with a delightful nuttiness that awakens your tongue as the cucumber cools and calms. The addition of sesame oil adds magical healing properties.

8 thick slices of cucumber

2 pinches of salt

1¾ oz (45 ml) blanco tequila

⅔ oz (20 ml) fresh lime juice

½ oz (15 ml) triple sec

¼ tsp sesame oil

Soda water, to taste

Garnish: cucumber slice

Serves 1

Muddle the cucumber with the salt in a shaker. Add the other ingredients except for the soda water and shake vigorously with ice. Fine-strain into a salt-rimmed tall glass (see page 13) and top up with soda water. Garnish with a long slice of cucumber.

Sesame Seed Scrying

A bag of sesame seeds holds much potential: the seeds are a food, their oil is healing, they abet protection magic, and they create wealth. Sesame seeds are small but mighty! They can even be used as a divination tool. Fill a bowl with sesame seeds and take it outside, ideally to a backyard patio or deck. Take a palmful of the seeds and throw them on the ground. Look carefully at the shape that is formed and take time to discern what you see. Is there a shape or a number, or a sign of a message? Do at least three readings in this way and make notes in your Book of Shadows (see page 15) on what you think the seeds are saying. You could even photograph the patterns and reflect upon them later. There will indeed be a message for the future.

Chapter 5

The Astrological Cocktail Guide

I rely upon my knowledge of astrology to guide many aspects of my life, including cocktails! Your astrological sign reveals much about your character and behaviors, and within this chapter you will find tips, spells, and rituals to enhance your best qualities. Your sun sign and ruling planets also influence your preferences in terms of what you enjoy, as well as the feeling and vibe you are looking for in witchy libations. Enjoy this celestial cocktail party!

Aries Dragon Heart

March 21–April 19

Of all the fire signs, Aries are the fieriest! Aries are the best at breaking down barriers, forging new paths, and pioneering in every imaginable way. This fire-breathing sign calls for a drink with dragon energy.

1 oz (30 ml) elderflower cordial

5 dashes aromatic bitters

3 lime wedges

1½ oz (45ml) aged rum

¾ oz (25 ml) mezcal

½ oz (15 ml) ginger liqueur

1½ oz (45 ml) blood orange juice

Garnish: blood orange peel

Serves 1

Put the elderflower cordial, bitters, and lime wedges into a cocktail shaker and muddle. Add the rum, mezcal, ginger liqueur, and blood orange juice, fill with ice, and shake. Strain into a chilled coupe glass. Garnish with the blood orange peel—cut into a flame shape, if you wish.

Crystal Flame Fire Agate Charm

Fire agate brings the wearer courage. If you are an Aries, make a fire agate your soul stone. Cleanse the stone by placing it in a bowl of rock salt overnight, then hold the fire agate with both hands and say:

Crystalline flame, from you, I draw power; stone of strength, I feel your might and force.

Into you, I instill my energy and intention.

I thank you, Mother Earth, for this great gift.

So mote it be!

Place it where you can see it every day, whether it is on your nightstand, altar, coffee table, or even desk or workspace.

Taurus Mystic Mulled Wine

April 20–May 20

Both sensual and sensible, practical and pragmatic, those born under the sign of the Taurus Bull are oftentimes excellent cooks, gardeners, parents, partners, and even can be gifted vintners if they so wish. A suitably simple recipe for Taurus hosts and oenophiles, this mulled wine recipe will please any palate.

750-ml bottle dry red wine

½ cup (125 ml) brandy

2 cinnamon sticks, cut into 3 pieces

1 tsp whole cloves

1 tsp whole allspice berries

1 large lemon peel

1 large orange peel

2 tbsp sugar

Garnish: cinnamon sticks

Serves 5

Combine the red wine, brandy, cinnamon sticks, cloves, allspice berries, lemon peel, and orange peel in a large saucepan over medium heat. Heat slowly until the mixture is warm—do not let it boil. Stir in the sugar and, once dissolved, taste to make sure you have the desired flavor.

Keep on low heat for 20 minutes to let the flavors infuse the wine. Serve your mulled wine hot in heatproof glasses or mugs. Garnish with a cinnamon stick.

Garden Your Way to Gladness

Taureans are blessed with green thumbs and love to garden; their gardens are usually bountiful and beautiful. Whether you're a Taurus or not, try planting happiness:

- For planting positive energy, plant hawthorn, heather, holly, hyacinth, hyssop, ivy, juniper, nasturtiums, or periwinkle.
- For healing, plant carnations, garlic, onions, peppermint, rosemary, sage, or sorrel.

Mai Tai Magic for Gemini

May 21–June 20

Two different kinds of rum, two different kinds of syrup, and two garnishes make this complex cocktail perfect for the Twins of the zodiac. The duality of ingredients satisfies the brilliance of Geminis, who abhor anything boring and prefer excitement, even in their drinks!

¾ oz (25 ml) fresh lime juice

1 oz (30 ml) orgeal syrup (rosewater)

1½ oz (45 ml) aged rum

½ oz (15 ml) orange liqueur, such as Grand Marnier

½ tsp simple syrup (see page 12)

½ oz (15 ml) dark rum

Garnish: fresh mint sprig, lime wedge

Serves 1

Add all the ingredients into a cocktail shaker except the dark rum. Add ice and shake until cold. Strain the cocktail into a highball glass filled with crushed ice. Top the drink with the dark rum, then garnish with a sprig of fresh mint and a lime wedge.

Mercury Bell Spell

Ruled by Mercury, Geminis can be gifted conversationalists, but their minds race. To calm this sign's busy brain, keep a small bell on your altar (see page 16) for a full week. Then, on a Wednesday, sit comfortably with the bell, ring it, and say:

As the sound of this bell now rings, I breathe in deeply, my heart takes wings.

Serenity and stillness and good things flow through me, my heart sings. And so it is!

Ring the bell once more, then sit in stillness and silence. Hold the feeling of tranquility and calm to get you through your busy days in the future.

Moonchild Moonwalk

June 21–July 22

Cancerians are fondly referred to as "moonchildren," since our beloved friends are born under the sign of the moon. This is why they are so sensitive, intuitive, and wise. This lovely lunar cocktail is suitable for any Cancerian.

5 drops orange flower water

5 drops grapefruit bitters

1 oz (30 ml) Grand Marnier

⅔ oz (20 ml) Champagne

1 cube white sugar

Champagne (approximately 3½ oz/100 ml), to top up

Garnish: orange twist

Serves 1

Put the orange flower water, grapefruit bitters, Grand Marnier, and ⅔ oz (20 ml) Champagne into a cocktail shaker with ice and stir. Put the sugar cube into a Champagne flute and strain the mixture over it. Top up with the Champagne. Mist the orange twist over the top, then gently drop it into the cocktail.

Moon Goddess Invocation

At the next full moon, make a promise to yourself to bring forth more self-love. Begin with a blissful bath in water scented with an essential oil such as bergamot, jasmine, or lavender. As you soak in the herb-infused water, speak this spell aloud:

I awaken the goddess in me. I embrace the power of the moon.

I call upon you, Lady of La Lune, to instill in me love and self-understanding.

I am alive! I am love! And so it is.

As you go through the days to come, notice your newfound glow of confidence and self-belief.

The Leo Sorceress

July 23–August 22

Leos call for a spectacular, unforgettable drink, such as this cocktail filled with drama, big and bold flavors, and a touch of the royal. Born under the sign of the lion, Leos are lovable and generous souls who have a talent for the dramatic they can often employ well in their careers.

1⅓ oz (40 ml) Hennessey Cognac

⅔ oz (20 ml) Campari

⅔ oz (20 ml) Gancia Rosso (Italian vermouth)

⅔ oz (20 ml) Cherry Heering

Garnish: slim orange wedge

Serves 1

Ideally serve this drink over triple-frozen ice (see page 10), which stays much colder than regular cubes. This means that the drink dilutes at a slower rate and remains at the ideal temperature for much longer. Combine all the ingredients in a mixing glass over ice. Stir for about 10 seconds, until the mixture is ice-cold, then strain into a small, chilled carafe. For presentation, pour the cocktail from the carafe into the glass (with ice and orange garnish in it) in front of the drinker.

Candle and Crystal Color Magic

Leos are associated with the sunny colors of gold, orange, yellow, and red but all lions should wield every color in the spectrum. Combining the intrinsic energy of sacred stones with candle color magic is a wonderful way to amplify the positive vibrations of your home sanctuary. Find what works best for you!

- Green candle and peridot or jade for creativity, prosperity, and growth.
- Orange candle and jasper or onyx for clear thinking and highest consciousness.
- Blue candle and turquoise or celestine for serenity, kindness, and a happy heart.
- White candle and quartz or limestone for purification and safety.

Mimosa Merriment for Virgos

August 23–September 22

This cocktail is light and features two healthful fruits. Simply bursting with antioxidants, this lovely sparkling drink is ideal for health-conscious Virgos. A toast to this intelligent and hard-working September sign!

1½ oz (45 ml) fresh orange juice

1½ oz (45 ml) pomegranate juice

4 oz (120 ml) Prosecco or a favorite Champagne

Garnish: rosemary sprig

Serves 1

Pour the juices into a Champagne flute. Now, tilt the flute and pour in the sparkling element of Prosecco or Champagne. Garnish with the rosemary sprig.

Make it a mocktail: Hold a Champagne flute at an angle and pour in 4 oz (120 ml) ginger ale. Top with 2 oz (60 ml) freshly squeezed orange juice. Saluté!

Powerful Herbal Amulets

Virgos usually have an affinity for herbalism. Fill a small cloth bag which can be tied closed with dried herbs or plants to take the protective energy of Mother Nature's protectors with you anywhere!

- For courage and heart: mullein or borage.
- For safe travels: comfrey.
- For protection from deceit: snapdragon.
- For good health: rue.
- For success: woodruff.
- For strength: mugwort.

Libra Angel

September 23–October 22

Artsy Libras strive for harmony and are seekers of truth and justice. Their sweetness and kindness make them a good friend to have, like having an angel in your corner—just like this angelic-looking cocktail.

1 oz (30 ml) Cointreau
2 oz (60 ml) gin
1 oz (30 ml) fresh lemon juice
1 egg white
Garnish: lemon slice
Serves 1

Pour the Cointreau, gin, lemon juice, and egg white into a cocktail shaker for a dry shake (without ice) for 15 seconds. Add ice to the shaker and shake for 30 seconds. Strain the mixture into a martini glass and after a few moments the egg white will create a frothy float at the top. Garnish with a lemon slice.

Sweetgrass Self-care Spell

Libras make being relaxed look easy, but being so supportive of others takes a great deal of effort. This self-care ritual helps maintain balance. Tie some sweetgrass leaves together, place them in a fireproof dish, light them, and pray:

This day I pray for peace, calm, health, and the wisdom to see the beauty and wonder of each waking moment.

Blessings abound for me and for those I love.

I pray for harmony in my heart and for this world.

And so it is!

Let the sweetgrass burn down completely as it purifies your space and calls forth angels, guardian spirits, and ancestors to you.

Scorpio Black Magic

October 23–November 21

Scorpios may well be misunderstood, but they might not mind as their reputation is also of being the sexiest of all the signs. With two kinds of bitters and a bold rye whiskey, this memorably mysterious cocktail fits Scorpio to a tee with the unusual combination of a strong taste that is also bracing and lingers long after you've finished.

2 oz (60 ml) rye whiskey

1 oz (30 ml) amaro liqueur

1 dash Angostura bitters

1 dash orange bitters

Garnish: cocktail cherry

Serves 1

Pour all the ingredients into a cocktail mixing glass. Add in 1 palmful of ice and stir for 30 seconds. Strain into a coupe glass and garnish with a cherry.

Scorpio Sensual Massage Oil

The way to make any Scorpio really happy is with sensual touch. I use this potion as a combination body-care oil and mystical massage oil. Add a pinch each of powdered clove, cinnamon, and ginger to 1 cup (250 ml) sesame oil in a small bowl. Add 1 drop of citrusy bergamot essential oil and 1 tsp each of amber and jasmine essential oil. Stir gently with a wooden spoon, then transfer to a dark blue or green sealable jar. Place the sealed jar beside a piece of magnetite, also known as lodestone, to instill the power of drawing people closer. Let it sit in a dry, dark cabinet for a full week, and then use the potion as a combination body-care oil and mystical massage oil to bring great pleasure into your life.

The Sagittarius Beatnik

November 22–December 21

Sagittarians love to explore, are indefatigable travelers, and are quite philosophical and intellectually curious; they seek spiritual heights and depths in their search for the ultimate meaning of life. The eternally cool Beatnik cocktail suits their thrill-seeking vibe.

½ oz (15 ml) tawny port

1 oz (30 ml) whiskey

1½ oz (45 ml) amaro liqueur

Garnish: flamed orange peel

Serves 1

Coat a martini glass with a few drops of the tawny port by swirling it thoroughly on the inside surface of the glass. Pour the rest of the port into an ice-filled cocktail shaker, then add the whiskey and the amaro. Shake until everything is well chilled. Strain into the prepared glass. Garnish with flamed orange peel (see page 12), allowing some of the oil from the orange peel to drop into the cocktail as it burns.

Travel Talisman Sagittarius Stone

Tourmaline—specifically the multihued specimen known as melonstone, which is pinkish-red with a blue-green stripe—is the precious soul stone for the Jupiter-ruled Sagittarians. Individuals under this fire sign are lively and very action-oriented, and tourmaline, which readily gives off an electrical charge when warmed, can match and propel their energy. Tourmaline is the stone for adventurers and explorers. Keep it in your pocket or wear it in a ring or necklace. Get some today and hit the road, dear Sagittarius!

Black Martini Mojo for Capricorns

December 22–January 19

Capricorns take life seriously and, as such, have earned a serious-looking cocktail. This dark and dramatic martini is ideal for ambitious goats who work very hard on their way up the mountain of success. This glamorous and dignified black martini is the drink they deserve!

2 oz (60 ml) frozen vodka, such as Stolichnaya

1 dash black sambuca

Serves 1

Pour the frozen vodka into a chilled martini glass, gently add the sambuca, and serve.

Intention Magic for Capricorns

Capricorns have an incredible will and discipline to meet their goals and make their dreams come true. I have Mars in Capricorn, which I see as one of the most important planetary placements in my astrology chart. For anything I have achieved, I credit that lucky star! Even with such self-control, Capricorns can use an aid for the mental and spiritual mindset that will abet attaining a vision for the future by setting intentions.

To choose a morning intention, decide what you want to achieve. Make sure your intention is positive, and shift any limiting beliefs. Then state your intention by vocalizing it or writing it down. Be clear and keep your intention simple. As an example, one of my recent intentions was: "I intend today's writing to flow easily, filled with inspiration that results in messages that help people and fill their hearts with happiness."

Aquarian Wild Irish Coffee

January 20–February 19

Legend has it that Irish Coffee was innovated on a wild and stormy night in 1942. The tempestuous origins of this cocktail make it perfect for Aquarians who like to work and play hard. This drink gives the energy of caffeine and the lift of Irish whiskey—the intensity water-bearers need.

1½ oz (45 ml) Irish whiskey, such as Jameson

⅔ oz (20 ml) simple syrup (see page 12)

3⅓ oz (100 ml) hot coffee

1 oz (30 ml) heavy (double) cream

Garnish: freshly grated nutmeg

Serves 1

Mix together the whiskey, simple syrup, and coffee in an Irish Coffee glass. Place the cream in a bowl and whisk until slightly thickened. Using a warm spoon, pour the cream over the top of the drink, creating a foamy "head." Garnish with freshly grated nutmeg.

Aquarius Mental Bliss Blend

Water-bearers make many demands of their intellect and mental energy. This deeply relaxing blend will allow their minds to rest and refresh. In a sealable blue or brown bottle, add 6 tbsp (90 ml) apricot oil to these essential oils: 20 drops sandalwood, 15 drops lavender, and 5 drops amber. Shake well. The oil keeps for 6 weeks.

Pour a little into the palm of your hand to warm before using. Rub it lightly onto your shoulder and neck, as well as your temples and wrists. Sit comfortably and breathe deeply with your eyes closed. Chant aloud:

Remove from me all worry. Remove all stress in a hurry.
No more will I lack sleep. No more will I weep.
Tranquility and calm, come to me now.

Pisces Absinthe Dream

February 20–March 20

Pisceans are the dreamiest of all the signs, as well as very psychic and imaginative. Absinthe contains herbs that inspire creativity and visions and have led to artistic breakthroughs, such as for Vincent van Gogh, who regularly imbibed the Green Fairy drink. This utterly unique cocktail is befitting the sign of the fishes, as they swim toward the deepest understanding of the universe.

1 oz (30 ml) absinthe

1 tsp simple syrup (see page 12)

4 oz (120 ml) Prosecco

Serves 1

Pour the absinthe and simple syrup into a V-shaped flute. Top with the Prosecco for a sparkling cocktail filled with mystery and magic.

Crystal Ball Divination

Every Pisces has the capacity for divining the truth—including the future. The ideal crystal ball for a Pisces would be made from their soul stone, amethyst, but any fine crystal ball can help in divining auguries. In a darkened room, sit and hold a crystal ball in the palms of both hands. Touch it to your heart and then gently touch it to the center of your forehead, where your third eye is located. Then hold the ball in front of your eyes and, sitting very still, gaze into it for at least three minutes. Envision pure white light in the ball and hold on to that image. What did you see? Shapes and shadows will form and flow, revealing the message. When we gaze into a crystal ball, it is possible to see into the fabric of time, both the past and the future. At first you may be able to see a flickering, wispy, suggestive image. Some of you may be able to see clearly defined visions on your first try. Take notes in your Book of Shadows (see page 15).

Chapter 6

Libations for Ritual Gatherings

Whether it is a high holiday or a humble family get-together, festive beverages add to the celebratory aspect of the occasion and bring people together in joy and appreciation of each other. How many times have you been to an event where, after you were introduced to a food, dessert, or drink that was completely new to you, you loved it and were asking for the recipe? I have experienced that many times, including several of the cocktails and mocktails in this book. Parties and group rituals are a wonderful way to share delightful treats with the special people in your life. These gatherings make our lives meaningful and will become memories you will treasure.

Aperol Sacred Spritz

I first drank this gorgeous cocktail at a women's writer fête at Zuni Café in San Francisco, a beloved spot. One of the very wise women ordered it and it was such a lovely color that I immediately requested one. A few days later, I bought all the ingredients and learned the art of the Aperol Spritz. I am thrilled to share it with you! It's light and bubbly, with hints of citrus and herbs: one of the most refreshing mixed drinks of all time.

2 oz (60 ml) chilled Aperol

3 oz (90 ml) chilled Prosecco

1 oz (30 ml) soda water

Garnish: orange wedge

Serves 1

Fill a white wine glass with ice. Pour the Aperol into the glass and stir. Top with the Prosecco and soda water. Gently squeeze the orange wedge into the glass and then stir the wedge into the drink. The color itself is pure magic!

New Moon Friday New Friends Spell

When I moved to San Francisco, I didn't know a soul, but I used this spell to fill my life with friends. On the first Friday (Freya's Day, ruled by Venus, is ideal for fun, love, flirtation, gossip, and good times) after a new moon, light some lavender incense. Anoint yourself with lavender essential oil and say aloud:

I call upon you, friend Freya, to fill my life with love and joy.

I call upon you, goddess, to bring unto me that which I enjoy in the form of people, wise and kind.

This I ask and give thanks for; blessed be.

When you go out for coffee or browse a bookstore or metaphysical shop, look around you: new friends may be right there, just a hello away!

Goddess Green Chartreuse

Chartreuse has a charming history. French monks worked with various combinations of herbs in the 1600s, and after decades arrived at this glorious green brew in 1764. It has many secret ingredients, but we do know it contains cinnamon, lemon balm, thyme, arnica flower, angelica root, hyssop, sage, and peppermint. Herbs are magic!

1 oz (30 ml) green Chartreuse liqueur

1 oz (30 ml) gin

1 oz (30 ml) maraschino liqueur

1 oz (30 ml) fresh lime juice

Garnish: cocktail cherries

Serves 1

Add all the ingredients into a cocktail shaker, then fill with ice and shake until cold. Strain into a coupe glass. Garnish with a couple of cocktail cherries.

Hedgewitch Hoedown

Be inspired by the industrious herbalist monks who steadfastly worked with these gifts from the earth to create blessed brews for health, comfort, and pleasure. Gardening is not a chore when you invite your fellow pagan pals for an outdoor party to sow seeds, do a little weeding, and plant herbs and flowers. Serve your guests a Goddess Green Chartreuse or another suitably herbal option, such as a Lavender Love Drop Mocktail (see page 132), and enjoy each other's good company and the generosity of Mother Earth! You can also say these words together:

Great Goddess of our Green Earth, we thank you today with heart and hands.

We pledge to preserve your beautiful land, and call all to join in the healing of our planet,

Ancient One, we thank you for your generosity.

With heart and hands, gratitude to you. Blessed be!

Shirley Temple Mocktail

When you think of mocktails, Shirley Temple is the first one that comes to mind. It is fizzy, fun, and a pleasing, pretty color. I will occasionally order one at a craft bar as a reminder of the elegance of simplicity. Whether you are 8 or 80 years old, this charmer will add a cherry on top of your day.

1 oz (30 ml) grenadine

½ oz (15 ml) fresh lime juice

5 oz (150 ml) ginger ale

Garnish: cocktail cherry

Serves 1

Add the grenadine and lime juice to a highball glass and stir. Add ice to the glass, leaving room at the top quarter of the glass. Top with the ginger ale. Garnish with a cocktail cherry.

A Gathering of the Tribe

Our lives are centered upon ritual. The Saturday night date is a romantic ritual, knitting circles are a growing trend, and doing yoga is replacing going to the gym as a spiritual and physical workout. People need ritual to inform and enrich their lives, to deal with stress, and to create meaning in their lives.

Family time should be a ritual too, whether it's a Wednesday night pizza, or more memorable events where every generation is present. A Shirley Temple Mocktail that everyone can enjoy is perfect for these special times! Enrich these moments further by adding a spiritual aspect—perhaps children could share the highlight of their week so far, and photos or memories could be added to a family album to be treasured for generations to come.

Juno's Gimlet

The strong and bright botanical aroma of gin is redolent of the juniper berries from which it is derived. Juno, wife of Jupiter and queen of the gods and goddesses, is the guardian deity for whom the berries are named. She is a protector to all women and she also lends favor to strong relationships and marriages.

½ oz (15 ml) fresh lime juice
2 oz (30 ml) gin (try Juno Gin!)
½ oz (15 ml) maple syrup
Soda water, to top up
Garnish: lime slice
Serves 1

Put the lime juice, gin, and syrup into a cocktail shaker, fill with ice, and shake until cold. Strain into a coupe glass and add a splash of soda water to top up. Garnish with a slice of lime.

Wedding Jubilee

One of my favorite trends of recent years is to have a hand-picked special craft cocktail at weddings. A Juno-blessed Gimlet would be a superb choice and bring her favor to your love and happy marriage. When everyone has a cocktail in hand, one of the wedding guests could make the following toast:

Here's to your long and joyous future together.
May it be filled with laughter, good cheer, and luck!
May you know contentment and a peaceful home.
Here's to every blessing in your marriage to come!
So mote it be.

As the glasses chime in toasting, make sure to be fully present in this moment of blissful happiness created by the power of love.

Strawberry Daiquiri Mocktail

This smoothie-like treat enchantment can be addictive as it is remarkably refreshing, bursting with healthful flavor and optimistic cheer. The strawberry-lime blend is especially welcome in hot weather.

2 cups (200 g) frozen strawberries

2 oz (60 ml) simple syrup (see page 12)

1½ oz (45 ml) fresh lime juice

1 cup (250 ml) lemon-lime soda

1 cup (200 g) ice

½ cup (125 ml) water

Garnish: fresh strawberries

Serves 1

Put everything apart from the water into a blender and blend until it is smoothly puréed. Stop blending, then add water a bit at a time and blend again until you have the desired consistency: not too thick but suitably drinkable. Pour into a glass and garnish with fresh strawberries.

New Witchy Friends Spell

Friends are some of the greatest loves of our lives. If you are looking to add new friends into your life, try this spell. Find a comfortable place to sit with a pink candle and two rose quartz crystals in front of you. Light the candles and say:

I light the fire of fellowship; in this candle, I see the flame of friendship.

Brightest blessing I now seek.

The spirit of friendship I welcome here, to share with me love, life, and light. And so it is!

Sit in a meditative state and ponder the qualities you want in your friends. Extinguish the candle, then place it and the two rose quartz crystals on your altar (see page 16). Repeat the spell every night until the pink candle has completely burned out, and new and interesting people will begin to enter your life.

Love Goddess Cosmopolitan

The combination of sweetness and tartness in this zesty beverage makes it very special, and the cranberry creates an irresistible party-pink color. It is ideal to serve at a goddess party dedicated to Venus.

1¼ oz (35 ml) lemon vodka

⅔ oz (20 ml) triple sec

⅔ oz (20 ml) fresh lime juice

1 oz (25 ml) cranberry juice

Garnish: flamed orange zest

Serves 1

Add all the ingredients to a cocktail shaker filled with ice cubes, shake sharply and strain into a chilled martini glass. Garnish with a flamed orange zest (see page 12) and serve.

Prayer to Venus: Love Goddess Incantation

The Roman goddess of love, Venus, is associated with ultimate femininity, sexuality, fertility, and beauty. The word veneration means to worship Venus, and one way to do that is have a Friday-night goddess party! Ask the women you invite to bring an offering of flowers, candles, and crystals. Light a candle on your altar (see page 16) in tribute to Venus and say the words of this invocation spell:

Beautiful goddess of love, we ask you to bless us with your bright energy.

We ask you to imbue us with your charm and grace.

We honor your power, in gratitude with love eternal.

Blessed be thee, so mote it be!

Spend time with your friends discussing how you want to express the love energy of Venus in your lives. When the rite is done, extinguish the candle. Enjoy the rest of your evening, sipping your Love Goddess Cosmopolitans! When everyone goes home, they should take an object from the altar that is not one they brought to keep on their nightstands to imbue their homes with the grace of Venus.

Beltane Mulata Daisy

The blend of fennel and chocolate liqueur in this cocktail creates a flavor profile that works superbly to awaken your taste buds and senses—perfect for Beltane, a celebration of pure sensuality!

⅓ oz (10 ml) Galliano liqueur

1 tsp superfine (caster) sugar

⅔ oz (20 ml) fresh lime juice

½ tsp fennel seeds

1⅓ oz (40 ml) rum, such as Bacardi

⅔ oz (20 ml) chocolate liqueur

Cocoa powder

Serves 1

Swirl the inside of the glass with the Galliano liqueur, which will give a bouquet of aniseed and other fresh aromas. Stir the sugar and lime juice together in a shaker; add the fennel seeds and muddle them gently with a stirrer. Add ice, the rum, and chocolate liqueur. Shake vigorously. Double-strain into a coupe glass with a cocoa powder rim (see page 13).

Beltane: May Day Celebration of Love

Beltane (April 30) is the witch's high holiday of love, observed with feasting and ceremonial ritual. After an all-night pagan lovefest, May Day is celebrated with dancing around a beribboned maypole. You can decide how you want your Beltane to go, as long as it is a fully sensual experience with food, dance, romance, and laughter. Ideally, celebrate May Day outdoors with your tribe. For those of us who don't have space for a maypole, represent the same spirit by asking attendees to bring colorful flowers to share on a table-turned-altar. When your tribe has arrived, recite this chant:

Hoof and horn, hoof and horn, tonight our spirits are reborn.

Welcome, joy, to my home.

Fill my friends with love and laughter.

So mote it be!

Make merry with your friends and share all the abundance and bounty of life with food, desserts, and drinks.

Bloody Mary Morning Mocktail

After a night of Beltane revelry, a hangover could well occur. The answer is a Bloody Mary: it has a near medicinal effect with its invigorating spices.

1 cup (250 ml) chilled virgin Bloody Mary mix

2 oz (60 ml) chilled tomato juice

⅓ oz (10 ml) fresh lemon juice

1 tsp Worcestershire sauce

2 tsp Tabasco hot sauce

2 tsp ready-for-use horseradish

1 tsp olive juice

½ tsp celery salt

1 pinch of black pepper

Garnish: celery stick

Serves 1

Pour the Virgin Bloody Mary mix into a small pitcher. Pour the cool tomato juice into a cocktail shaker and shake. Add all the remaining ingredients and "dry shake" (without ice). Strain into the pitcher and stir until well mixed. Serve in a salt-rimmed glass (see page 13) and garnish with a celery stick.

Prosecco Mary

A traditional non-virgin Bloody Mary features vodka, but you can change it up by adding Prosecco as well.

1 oz (30 ml) vodka

2½ oz (75 ml) tomato juice

1 dash Tabasco hot sauce

1 pinch of sugar

¼ tsp smoked water (optional)

About 2½ oz (75 ml) chilled Prosecco

Garnish: cucumber ribbon

Serves 1

Pour the vodka, tomato juice, Tabasco, sugar, and smoked water (if liked) into a cocktail shaker half-filled with ice cubes. Shake vigorously and pour into a flute. Add half the Prosecco and stir gently to combine. Top up with the rest of the Prosecco. Garnish with a cucumber ribbon.

Lavender Love Drop Mocktail

To me, lavender is love in herbal form. It's useful in so many ways, from a calming tea to soothe anxiety and in healing salves, to beautifying your garden and cleansing your sacred space. Adding the mild and slightly peppery flavor of lavender to a mocktail makes for a magical drink to serve at ritual gatherings.

1 cup (250 ml) fresh lemon juice

1 cup (250 ml) Lavender Simple Syrup (see below)

3 cups (750 ml) cold water

Serves 4

Pour the lemon juice into a medium-sized pitcher. Add the Lavender Simple Syrup, followed by the water, and stir. Top the pitcher with ice and serve.

For the Lavender Simple Syrup: Add ¼ cup (10 g) dried lavender blossoms (choose blossoms dried for culinary use), ½ cup (125 ml) water, and ½ cup (125 g) sugar to a small saucepan and heat slowly on medium heat. Bring to a simmer and stir, until the sugar is fully dissolved. Turn off the heat and let sit for 20 minutes. When it reaches room temperature, strain it into a sterilized sealable jar and refrigerate. The syrup will keep for up to 1 month.

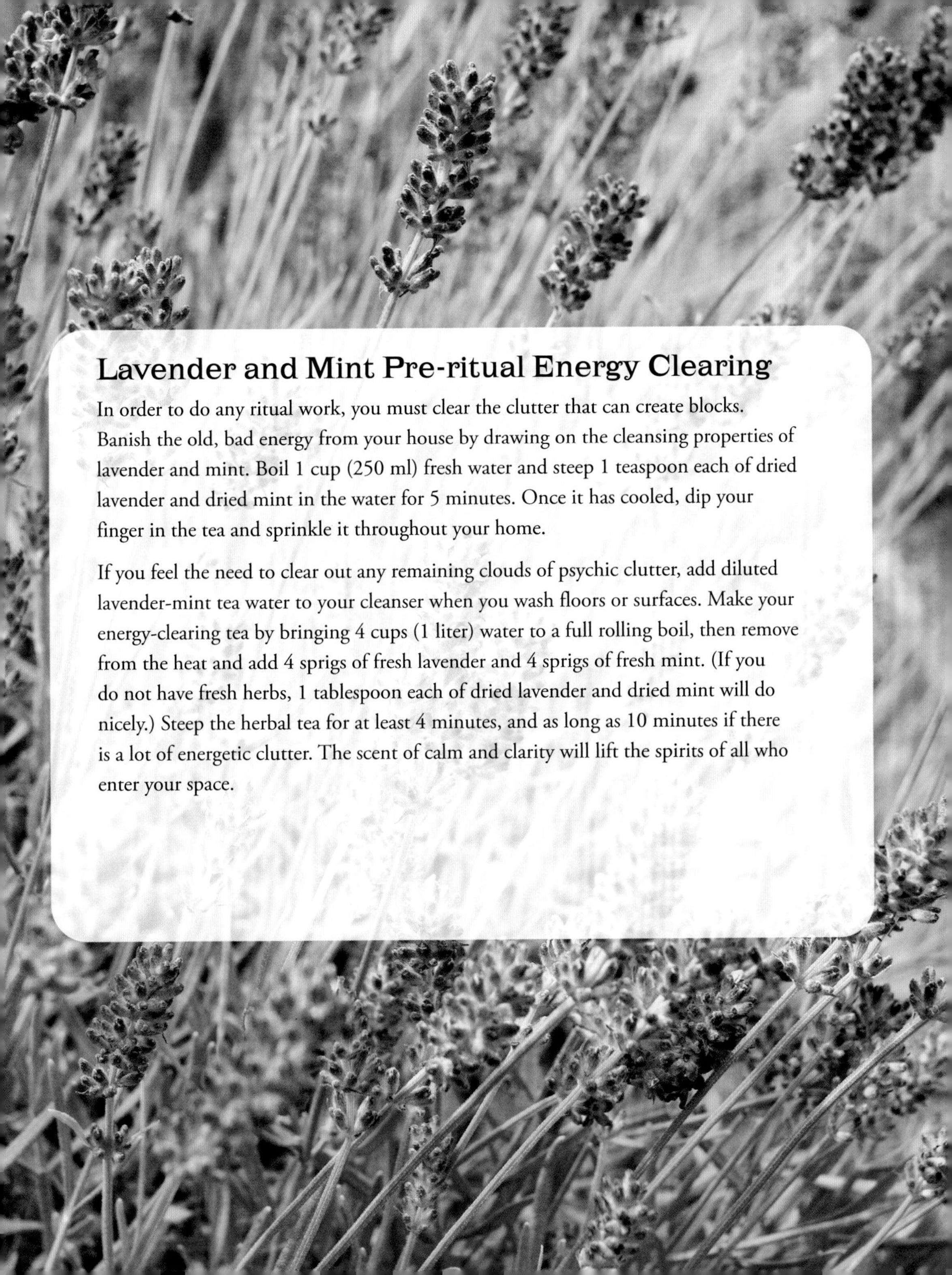

Lavender and Mint Pre-ritual Energy Clearing

In order to do any ritual work, you must clear the clutter that can create blocks. Banish the old, bad energy from your house by drawing on the cleansing properties of lavender and mint. Boil 1 cup (250 ml) fresh water and steep 1 teaspoon each of dried lavender and dried mint in the water for 5 minutes. Once it has cooled, dip your finger in the tea and sprinkle it throughout your home.

If you feel the need to clear out any remaining clouds of psychic clutter, add diluted lavender-mint tea water to your cleanser when you wash floors or surfaces. Make your energy-clearing tea by bringing 4 cups (1 liter) water to a full rolling boil, then remove from the heat and add 4 sprigs of fresh lavender and 4 sprigs of fresh mint. (If you do not have fresh herbs, 1 tablespoon each of dried lavender and dried mint will do nicely.) Steep the herbal tea for at least 4 minutes, and as long as 10 minutes if there is a lot of energetic clutter. The scent of calm and clarity will lift the spirits of all who enter your space.

Summer Celebration Chalice

This cocktail contains the very spirit of summer and will make any gathering memorable, especially a celebration of the solstice. The alchemy of the fruits with the sparkling Champagne and elderflower combines in such a way that it is a rapturous libation.

5 oz (150 ml) Champagne

1 strawberry, cut into 4 pieces

1 blackberry

2 raspberries

2 tsp (10 ml) elderflower liqueur

⅔ oz (20 ml) rhubarb liqueur

Serves 1

Fill a wine glass two-fifths full with Champagne. Add three cubes of ice, then the fruit and the liqueurs. Top up with more ice and more Champagne.

Make it a mocktail: Use nonalcoholic sparkling cider instead of Champagne.

Summer Solstice Morning Rite

The celebration of the longest day (June 21) starts at dawn. Ask those attending to bring food and drink and to wear festive, colorful, and exuberant garb. All present should weave garlands of flowers as the sun slowly rises. When the sun is just fully visible, the host should direct the gathered celebrants to form a circle. The host should pray aloud:

This sun festival is now begun under this longest day of the sun.

Let us go forth and make merry.

The god and goddess are here!

Then all say:

Blessed be!

As you watch the sun rise, think of its awesome power, and enjoy sharing the food and drinks—including Summer Celebration Chalice cocktails or mocktails!

Summer Sotol Margarita

Unlike mezcal and tequila, which are made from agave, Sotol is made from a flowering shrub known as the Desert Spoon. This plant restores the earth in which it grows, so makes for a more sustainable ingredient.

1¾ oz (50 ml) Sotol, such as La Higuera

¾ oz (25 ml) Vault Aperitivo de Agave

½ oz (15 ml) Cointreau

Garnish: lemon peel twist

Serves 1

Stir the ingredients thoroughly with ice in a mixing glass and strain into a classic martini glass. Garnish with a twist of lemon peel.

Season of Summer Ritual

Invite your coven over on a sunny Saturday. Set up a table and chairs as an altar (see page 16) in your backyard or even use a picnic table in a local park. Cover with a colorful, flowery cloth. Place an image of Persephone (harbinger deity of the summer season) in the middle of the altar, with incense in a fireproof dish. Bring a big cauldron filled with water for flower offerings. Ask your coven to each bring an offering such as fruit, candles, crystals, herbs, or seashells, along with food and drinks to share, and ingredients for your Summer Sotol Margaritas for those who wish to partake! Include a beautiful pomegranate to also represent Persephone.

Gather everyone around the altar, light the incense and candles, and start the ritual by holding the pomegranate and stating your intentions for the summer season. When you have finished speaking, say:

And so it is. Blessed be!

Pass the pomegranate to the next woman so she can say her sacred intentions. Every person should end with the same words that seal the magic. When everyone has spoken, feasting should begin, along with discussion of your visions for the future. Be sure every woman eats pomegranate seeds in honor of Persephone.

Harvest Moon Apple Sangria

Sangria is meant to be shared and savored while relaxing with friends. This cool classic is fantastic for summer seasonal rites such as Midsummer, Lammas Day, and Autumnal Equinox.

1 red apple, sliced
1 green apple, sliced
3 tbsp (35 g) sugar
½ tsp ground cinnamon
1 lemon, sliced
750-ml bottle chilled dry red wine
½ cup (125 ml) brandy
3 cinnamon sticks
Apple cider, to top up

Serves 5

Place the apple slices in the bottom of a pitcher, add the sugar and ground cinnamon, and stir. Set the pitcher aside for 15 minutes at room temperature. Pour the red wine into the pitcher, along with the brandy, cinnamon sticks, and lemon slices. Stir until well mixed then refrigerate for 2 hours. Fill tall serving glasses with ice, pour in the sangria, and add a splash of apple cider to top up.

Singing Moon Harvest Rite

The full moon of September is the Harvest Moon, also known as the Singing Moon, and is the perfect time for creating a gratitude altar in honor of the bounty we all enjoy. Arrange pumpkins, acorns, branches, and leaves to represent autumn's natural changes. Gather guests around the altar and share bread, cheeses, fruits, and newly harvested vegetables. The fragrant sangria is precisely right as an accompaniment. Pour a toast to the season, then say:

Harvest is here and the seasons do change: this is the height of the year.

The bounty of summer sustains us in spirit, soul, and body.

Gratitude to the deities, and thankfulness to farmers and vintners whose bounty we share in love and joy.

And so it is!

Miracle Madras

This bracing Samhain cocktail celebrates two of Mother Nature's great gifts of northern climes: cranberry and maple syrup. The maple essence is a mighty antioxidant and is also good for money magic, love spells, and wellbeing rituals, in which it abets longevity. To your health!

1½ oz (45 ml) vodka

2 oz (60 ml) unsweetened cranberry juice

1 tsp maple syrup

1½ oz (45 ml) fresh orange juice

1 lime wedge

Garnish: lime wedge

Serves 1

Fill a highball glass with ice. Add the vodka, cranberry juice, and maple syrup, and stir with a barspoon. Pour in the orange juice and add in one squeeze of a wedge of lime. Garnish with a fresh lime wedge as the finishing touch.

Sacred Samhain Spell

October 31, the Wiccan New Year's Eve, is truly one of the most important nights of the year when the veil is thinnest between worlds, making Samhain the time to honor and connect with ancestors, loved ones, and spirits on the other side. Create a simple altar with the bounty of the season, such as apples, pears, pumpkins, cranberries, and pomegranates as offerings. Burn potent incense in a fireproof dish which connects with spirits on the other side and calls them forth. Light a white candle and intone aloud:

On this hallowed night, we honor those who came before.

We look to the New Year for new beginnings.

May all be guarded, guided, and protected! Blessed be!

Toast the ancestors, gods, and goddesses with your Miracle Madras cocktail and savor the drink as you contemplate the boundless blessings on this holiest of nights.

Solstice Hot Spiced-tini

Winter gatherings call for a heart- and soul-warming libation like this. The pleasing spiciness brings both cheer and comfort. No matter how chilly the night, this beautiful blend of spirits will lend conviviality.

1¾ oz (50 ml) aged gin, such as Booth's or Campfire

⅔ oz (20 ml) Montenegro amaro

⅓ oz (10 ml) red vermouth, such as Sacred English Spiced

3–4 dashes Angostura bitters

2 oz (60 ml) hot water (not boiling)

Garnish: orange peel, star anise

Serves 1

Preheat a brandy balloon glass with warm water (hot faucet/tap water is fine). Add all the ingredients to a heatproof pitcher and stir (without ice), then gently pour the mix into the brandy balloon. Garnish with a piece of orange peel and a star anise.

Winter Solstice Ritual

Winter solstice (December 21) rituals celebrate the rebirth of the sun. In a safe place outdoors, build a bonfire as a warm and welcoming atmosphere to receive guests. If it is too cold or snowy where you live, gather indoors and form a semicircle around the fireplace. Create a solstice altar to the east of the fire by placing a small cauldron there with a candle in it surrounded by mistletoe, ivy, and holly. Participants should also wear crowns woven from these evergreens. Once guests are comfortably gathered round, say aloud so all can hear:

Brigid, Diana, Freya, Cerridwen, Heaven's Queen,

By the light of this moon in this dark night,

Blessed be to the Mother Goddess!

Thank you for the sun that gives us life!

Now toast to the new sun with a Solstice Hot Spiced-tini and other hot and hearty drinks. Savor the fellowship of like-minded folks, the coziness of the fire, and good spirits!

Index

Credits

Image Credits

All photography/illustrations © Ryland Peters and Small/CICO Books except as otherwise stated.

Photography

Stephen Conroy: pages 1, 2, 3, 3, 8, 11, 13, 31, 35, 55, 69, 76, 79, 89, 101, 118, 123, 139; **Caroline Arber:** page 83; **Peter Cassidy:** page 66; **Belle Daughtry:** page 14; **Georgia Glynn-Smith:** page 20; **Cath Gratwicke:** page 17; **Gavin Kingcome:** pages 10, 107, 134; **Erin Kunkel:** pages 21, 22, 23; **Adrian Lawrence:** page 117; **Kim Lightbody:** pages 24, 28, 43, 61, 127; **William Lingwood:** pages 56, 80, 83, 102; **Alex Luck:** pages 27, 36, 38, 41, 47, 48, 51, 52, 62, 65, 75, 86, 90, 93, 97, 98, 113, 114, 120, 131, 140; **Steve Painter:** pages 70, 84; **Roy Palmer:** pages 18, 100, 111; **Lucinda Symons:** page 133; **© AdobeStock/bellakadife:** page 67.

Illustrations

© AdobeStock/Rahmat: tree branches throughout; **© AdobeStock/Kirill:** sun and moon on pages 4, 5, 19, 26, 30, 40, 46, 54, 68, 78, 88, 96, 100, 112, 122, 138; **© AdobeStock/shabana:** decorative borders on pages 32, 37, 38, 39, 44, 45, 58, 63, 66, 72, 73, 74, 84, 85, 94, 95, 103, 104, 105, 108, 109, 110, 111, 124, 125.

Recipe Credits

Brenda Knight (Cerridwen Greenleaf): pages 30–31, 32, 33, 34–35, 39, 54–55, 59, 68–69, 73, 78–79, 84, 85, 88–89, 100–101, 104, 108, 109, 110, 111, 112–113, 122–123, 132–133, 137, 138–139; **Julia Charles:** pages 45, 46–47, 90–91, 130–131; **Leigh Clarke:** pages 64–65, 66–67; **Jesse Estes:** pages 36–37, 72, 114–115; **Laura Gladwin:** pages 60–61, 82–83, 116–117, 120–121; **Hannah Miles:** pages 70–71; **Lottie Muir:** pages 42–43, 126–127; **Louise Pickford:** pages 80–81, 95; **Ben Reed:** pages 48–49, 50–51, 56–57, 102–103, 124, 125, 128; **David T. Smith & Keli Rivers:** pages 38, 40–41, 62–63, 74–75, 86–87, 92–93, 94, 96–97, 136, 140–141; **William Yeoward:** pages 44, 58, 105, 106–107, 129, 134–135, plus some text on pages 10 and 12–13.

Acknowledgments

I am always grateful to CICO for the opportunity to work on books that are a joy to write and, I sincerely hope, are an equal joy to read. This tome was a true collaboration with editors Kristine Pidkameny and Carmel Edmonds, who did a lot of the heavy lifting to bring this book together. I will forever be thankful to them for that. The stylist, photographer, and design team outdid themselves on this stunning volume. A toast to CICO Books!